PSYCHOLOGY
OF
CHILDHOOD

FOR

STUDENTS OF CHILD PSYCHOLOGY
PARENTS
TEACHERS

by

LESTER D. CROW, Ph.D.; L.H.D.; LL.D.; Litt.D.
Professor of Education Emeritus
Brooklyn College of City University of New York

1981

Printed in the United States of America
by Prinit Press, Dublin, Indiana 47335

Copyright © by Lester D. Crow, 1981

I.S.B.N. 0-932970-24-9

Manufactured in the United States of America
by
Prinit Press, Dublin, Indiana 47335

TABLE OF CONTENTS

The Science of Child Study

Child psychology is a scientific study of the individual from his prenatal beginnings through the early stages of his adolescent development. The science of child psychology deals with (1) the stages of growth and maturation, (2) the effects of environmental influences upon individual patterns of development, and (3) the psychological and social interactions between a child and the other members of the society into which he is born and in which he is reared.

Before birth and thereafter, a continuing interrelationship exists between the child and society. Certain factors of growth are more or less common for all individuals. These can be treated separately, although constant attention must be given to (1) the interrelationships that exist among the child's various phases of growth and (2) the interrelationships between the child and the environmental influences by which he is surrounded, to which he responds and which he himself may affect as he develops his behavior potentialities.

SIGNIFICANCE OF CHILD STUDY

Psychologists, parents, teachers, and other adults who are interested in the welfare of both the individual and society have become increasingly aware of the significance of the childhood years of the individual. Phrases such as "he child is father of the man" and "the first six years of life are the most important" attest to the existing interest in child development.

At one time children were regarded as miniature adults. During the era of Puritan rigidity, children were "to be seen but not heard." Young children were thought to have little or no need for any except physical care. The fact is now recognized that, during all the stages of his growth, a child requires intelligent care of his physical needs and trained guidance of his mental, emotional, and social potentialities.

Too often, abnormalities of adolescent or of adult behavior can be traced to insufficient care during the childhood years, accompanied by the development of undesirable attitudes and behavior patterns. Case histories of the mentally ill or of criminals disclose the fact that inadequate parental understanding and care, childhood conflicts and frustrations, failure to progress in school, or unsatisfying social relationships with peers or adults result in later personal and social maladjustments.

Child study, in and of itself, will not guarantee that a child thus studied will develop a completely acceptable pattern of adult behavior. Too many factors affect the life of the child to make this possible. Moreover, we still do not have sufficient scientific knowledge concerning the psychology of human development and human interaction to predict with certainty that any recommended program of child care and rearing will achieve expected results in terms of adult attitudes and behavior. As methods of study are improved, however, and the results of these studies are applied in the guidance of child development, it can be hoped that an increasing number of children will grow and develop under conditions that are more conducive to greater physical and mental health and to better social interrelationships.

PREFACE

Child psychology is a subject that is of interest and value to parents, teachers and students. This discussion is concerned with helping the reader better to understand the behavior and development of the child from birth to adolescence. The many facets of the child's personality are explored during his progressive patterns of growth and development. Throughout the book, attention is given to the maturation of the child as his development is influenced by the environment.

The treatment includes the beginnings of life, including biological inheritance and prenatal development and, the anatomical and physiological factors of growth and development. Basic consideration also is given to motor and mental abilities, emotional behavior and the development of self-discipline. Attention is given to the child's creative activity and the dynamics of child behavior together with the sexuality of childhood and the adjustment problems faced during the developing years. These are presented in such a way as to help the reader gain a better understanding of the behavior problems of the developing individual.

In order to avoid excessive use of the pronouns *he, she, his, him* or *her,* I have used the masculine form, where applicable, to include the members of both sexes.

Finally, this book was written, not only for the purpose of being helpful to students in courses in child psychology, but also to assist parents, teachers and everyone concerned with the problem of better understanding child behavior during his or her growing years.

June, 1981   Lester D. Crow

CHAPTER 1

The Beginnings of Life

A child's developmental pattern is influenced by two general sets of factors: (1) the inheritance of anatomical and physical characteristics and behavior potentialities through the germ cells of the child's parents, and (2) the effect upon the child from conception onward of the multitudinous influences by which he is surrounded. The relative significance of biological inheritance as compared with what might be termed social heritage is a moot question. It is a fact that in a single cell are contained the beginnings of life. Whatever happens to this cell in its course of growth and development will determine the kind of person that finally emerges.

THE GENERAL NATURE OF GROWTH AND DEVELOPMENT

The currently accepted *organismic* concept of development is based upon the theory that all phases or aspects of development must be interpreted in respect to a life pattern. Concern is with the *total* child, rather than with isolated phases of his development. For example, the individual's physical growth and development do not progress apart from other aspects of his developing personality. There is a constant interaction among the various aspects of the child's life experiences.

Growth versus Development. The exact connotation of each of the two terms — *growth* and *development* — is not always explained clearly, even in scientific literature. Sometimes the terms are used synonymously. At other times, the term *growth* is applied to maturation, and *development* is applied to changes brought about by environmental influences, or learning. According to another viewpoint, by *development* is meant the perspective of change in the total organism, whereas *growth* connotes change in a particular phase or partial aspect, although change in any one aspect is related to other changes that are taking place within the total organism. The last-named interpretation of the terms *growth* and *development* is, in general, the one to which the authors subscribe.

Principles of Growth. As a child grows, both quantitative and qualitative changes are taking place within him. Although reference often is made to "norms" of growth, the growth pattern of any one child is different from that of every other child. Growth curves in any aspects of development may show some similarity, but they also indicate differences in rate, extent, and variability of development.

Regardless of the maximum of growth attained in any aspect of development, growth is continuous within its limitations of extent. The overt expression of growth may not always be observable, but changes are constantly taking place within the individual which, in some instances, may seem to show themselves suddenly and without warning.

Since growth is influenced by many environmental factors, progress in any area of development is modifiable. Whether the modification of the growth pattern is favorable depends upon the kind of environmental stimulations to which the individual is exposed and the interactions between these stimulations and inherent constitution.

Maturation follows a course that limits the responsive behavior of a child at his various stages of growth. No amount or kind of external stimulation can force natural limits. Within these maturational limits, however, much can be done through the provision of favorable learning situations to facilitate growth in any aspect of development.

BIOLOGICAL INHERITANCE

Life begins with the union of one cell (the ovum) from the mother with one cell (the sperm) from the father. Because of its complexity many aspects of human heredity are not yet fully understood. It is known that the fertilized cell contains twenty-three pairs of chromosomes, one of each pair contributed by the father and the other by the mother. Within each of these threadlike bodies can be found hundreds of invisible particles called *genes.* These genes control hereditary traits. Individual differences among native traits which appear even in the children of the same parents can be explained in terms of variation in the organization of the genes of the fertilized cell.

Principles of Biological Inheritance. As far as we know, biological inheritance functions in a very general way as follows:

1. The maturational pattern is generally similar for each species or genus respectively. Hence, all human beings have many characteristics in common.

2. Although many human traits are biologically inherited, others develop as a result of environmental influences. The extent to which heredity plays any part in environmentally acquired traits has not yet been determined.

3. Specific characteristics of the new organism result from various combinations of genes present in the fertilized cell. The element of chance makes impossible, or almost so, any completely adequate prediction concerning the quality of the characteristics developing within the new organism.

4. Of the child's total inheritance, 50 per cent is contributed by the child's maternal line and 50 per cent by the paternal line. The mother contributes twenty-three *x* chromosomes, the child will be a female. If he contributes twenty-two *x* and one *y*, the child will be a male.

Not all the child's characteristics are inherited directly from the immediate parents. In general, it can be estimated that one-half of his traits come from his parents, one-fourth from his grandparents, one-eighth from his great-grandparents, and lesser fractions proportionately down the ancestral line. Members of the same family tend to be more like one another than members of unrelated families, but significant differences occur among siblings, except in the case of identical twins (a fertilized ovum splitting into two separate cells).

5. Certain genes appear to be stronger than others. The traits produced by *dominant* genes are more likely to appear than are those that might be produced by the weaker or *recessive* genes. The theory of dominance and recessiveness of inheritance traits was first propounded by Mendel in 1866, with publication of the results of his experiments in the hybridization of peas.

Significance of Biological Inheritance. The study of a child of

3

any age usually begins with the characteristics that he displays at the time of the study. In order to understand more fully, however, the underlying reasons for his present health and physical status, attitudes, and behavior patterns, one must study the background history of the child as well as the environment in which he lives. Hence, it is important to know something about the child's "family tree" and to discover which characteristics are explainable in terms of biological inheritance. Since not too much is known concerning the relative influence of heredity and environment, sweeping conclusions must be avoided.

Physical Characteristics. In general, there can be found family resemblances in physical structure. Tall parents tend to have tall children, although the offspring may be either somewhat taller or shorter than the parents. The same principle holds in the matter of short stature. Bony structure, weight, hair and eye color, and formation of features may follow a more or less general family pattern. Color blindness and hemophilia (excessive bleeding) also seem to be among inheritable physical traits. So far as is known from present evidence, changes in the somatic cells acquired by parents during their lifetime are not inheritable.

Mental Characteristics. A child's demonstrated degree of mental alertness at any stage of his development can be traced to many sources, including the kind and amount of environmental stimulation that he receives. There is evidence, resulting from many research studies, that inherited capacity for mental activity is a potent factor in the mental development of the child. Above-average mental acuity seems to "run" in families, although the extent to which this can be traced to favorable conditions in the homes of mentally superior parents is debatable. It has been demonstrated that certain types of feeble-mindedness are inherited. However, not all mental subnormality or even slowness of mental reaction can be explained in this way.

Modern research has exploded the theory that insanity is always an inherited characteristic. A few kinds of mental disorder, such as Huntington's chorea, are believed to be inheritabl. Most forms of mental illness have their roots in organic disorders, or are functional to the extent that an individual may have inherited a constitution that is especially susceptible to the effects of severe stresses and stains.

Disease. Contrary to earlier beliefs, it is probable that few, if any, diseases are inherited. An inherited constitutional weakness

4

may cause an individual to be susceptible to diseases such as tuberculosis, cancer, diabetes, diphtheria, and rheumatic heart condition. Gonorhea and syphilis are not inherited but may be transmitted either before or at birth to the child by an infected mother. An environment conducive to physical and mental health and a high degree of emotional stability are excellent preventives against most diseases.

PRENATAL DEVELOPMENT

Child psychologists are attaching considerable importance to the kind of development that takes place during the prenatal period. The methods employed to study the unborn child's rate and kind of development are rapidly improving. Included among generally utilized methods are: observation of fetuses that have been removed surgically from the mother's body; observation of infants who have been born prematurely but who survive; and observation of the activities of the fetus by means of the use of a special apparatus that is attached to the abdomen of the mother. Although these techniques are not completely adequate, they are affording scientists the opportunity to learn more about this early period of development than was possible in the past.

The normal prenatal period of the human being is approximately nine calendar months or about 270 days in length. During this period, the new life which began as a single fertilized cell passes through a remarkable process of development. By the time the child is ready to be born, he normally possesses all the potentialities of adequate postbirth growth and development. Environmental influences (circumscribed as they may be) affect the unborn child's development in much the same way as they do postbirth development.

There are known to be three roughly divided periods of prenatal development: (1) the *germinal* period or the period of the ovum, extending from the moment of fertilization to about the end of the second week; (2) the *embryonic* period or the period of the embryo, beginning at the end of the second week and extending to about the end of the second month after fertilization; (3) the *fetal* period or the period of the fetus, extending from about the end of the second month of prenatal life to birth.

The Germinal Period. During the germinal period, the *zygote* or fertilized egg is not attached to the mother but floats freely,

5

receives little or no nourishment, and maintains an egglike appearance, with little if any change in size. Important changes are going on within the internal structure. The original single cell divides and subdivides many times and at a rapid rate. Finally a cluster of globules forms. This cluster contains many cells. Each new cell contains a set of all the original genes. A small cavity that forms within the cell mass produces two separated clusters of cells, one outer and the other inner. The embryo later is formed from part of the inner cluster. The outer cluster becomes the protective and nourishing tissues of the embryo.

As the cell division is taking place, the ovum passes down the Fallopian tube to the uterus, which meanwhile has undergone changes in structure. Upon reaching the uterus, the ovum attaches itself to the uterus wall. At the point of implantation, the placenta (from which the umbilical cord extends to the ovum) develops. In this way the ovum receives nourishment from the blood stream of the mother.

The Embryonic Period. Many changes take place rapidly during the embryonic period. The cell mass divides into three germ layers: the outer layer or *ectoderm* which produces the nervous system, sensory cells, skin, glands, hair and nails, parts of the teeth, and the epidermis of the skin; the middle layer or *mesoderm* which produces the circulatory and excretory organs, the muscles, and the inner layer of the skin or dermis; the innermost layer or *endoderm* which produces the Eustachian tube, bronchia, trachea, lungs, pancreas, liver, the lining of the digestive tract, the salivary glands, and the thyroid gland and thymus. At the end of this period the organism exhibits the beginnings of the appearance of a human being, and the potentialities of behavior are in the making.

The placenta continues to grow until, within six months, it covers about half the uterus. The functions of this membrane include the protection of the embryo; the passage of water, oxygen, and nutriments from the mother's blood to the embryo by means of the umbilical cord; and the disposal of waste products from the embryo through the mother's blood stream. At no time is there any direct connection between the blood stream of the mother and that of the developing child.

The heart has begun to function by the end of the third week. During the second month some of the organs, such as the liver, begin to function. The direction of embryonic development is from the head down and from the trunk outward.

6

Embryonic development as described briefly in the foregoing represents normal growth of a healthy zygote in a healthful environment. If conditions are not favorable to growth and development, the fertilized ovum will not survive.

The Fetal Period. In general, the fetal period is that in which the growth and development begun during the emryonic period are continued. The various organs gradually begin to function much in the way that will be characteristic of the infant. The heart takes on a rhythmic beat, the fetus grows in size, and spontaneous movements of various parts of the body are possible. There also is some sensory development before birth, and feeble crying may be experienced as early as the fifth or sixth month. Relatively little is known, however, concerning prenatal development of the nervous system.

Congenital Inheritance. Various factors can influence prenatal development. Superstitions such as the notion that a mother can "mark" her unborn baby through one or another form of thought transference have been largely discounted by scientists. It is not yet possible to explain all the abnormalities of development that may occur during this period of development, but scientific study is progressing rapidly in this direction.

Certain undesirable influences that are not inherent in the germ plasm affect the individual during the prenatal period. These are referred to generally as factors of *congenital inheritance*. Congenital experiences resulting from the mother's physical condition that may be unfavorable to normal prenatal development are: toxic poisoning, disease, malnutrition, infection, endocrine imbalance, and possibly a severe nervous shock. To these can be added birth injuries that may result in feeble-mindedness or other abnormalities.

THE NEWBORN INFANT

Germinal and congenital inheritance, the condition of the mother during gestation (pregnancy), and possibly the hormone oxytoxin produced by the placenta may be some of the factors that determine when parturition, or the birth of the baby, will take place. Although the normal length of time from conception to parturition is accepted to be any time from 267 to 280 days, there are cases in which normal birth has occurred either earlier or later. The time itself is not significant; the birth experience and its

7

consequent effects upon the mother and the child are the important factors.

The Birth Experience. There usually are three successive stages in labor (birth pains): (1) the period of dilation from the start of the labor pains until the cervix of the uterus is fully dilated; (2) the stage of expulsion, during which time the contraction of the uterine muscles results in the fetus being expelled from the uterus; and (3) the placental stage during which the placenta and membranes are expelled. The length of time involved in each one of the stages varies. For a woman's first birth, the first period may last from twelve to twenty hours, the second from one to four hours, and the third an hour or less. The total time usually is less for women who have given birth to several children.

A child may be born in any one of several ways. The most usual method is the *vertex presentation,* wherein the child passes head first through the birth canal. The *transverse presentation* is a form of delivery employed when the fetus lies crosswise in the uterus of the mother. In this form of delivery there is danger that the child may suffocate because of the delay in bringing his head out of the canal. This situation exists also in *breech presentation,* in which the child's buttocks appear before the legs and the head. It is possible, however, for the obstetrician to change the position of the fetus so as to insure a normal birth.

Another type of delivery, called *Caesarean section,* is surgical delivery through the abdominal wall of the mother. This method is not utilized except when the mother's health or the smallness of her organs would seem to make a normal delivery inadvisable. The developmental status need not be affected thereby.

Although not scientifically established, it is believed that the birth experience causes the newborn child to suffer a condition of shock from which he may recover only gradually during his first days of life. Some writers have attempted to find in this traumatic experience, especially if the obstetrician has difficulty with his instruments, the roots of later inadequacies and maladjustments.

Characteristics of the "Just Born." The first cry of the newborn, either spontaneous or externally induced, probably represents the beginning of independent respiration. The newborn baby's body appears to be very much out of proportion as compared with adult standards. His bones are pliable and cartilaginous. The skull contains six soft spots (fontanels) that are membranes connecting the more ossified areas.

At birth, respiration is abdominal and ranges in rate from about thirty-two respirations per minute to a hundred or more during violent crying. On the average, defecations number about four or five during a twenty-four-hour period and urinations are about eighteen or nineteen for the same length of time. Even at the moment of birth, a child may give some slight evidence of awareness of his environment.

THE NEONATE

A child born after a full-time prenatal period usually is referred to as a *full-term neonate* for about the first four weeks of his postnatal life. During this period, the infant is attempting to adjust himself to his new environment. The full-term neonate is equipped to make the transition from the sheltered environment of his mother's body to the outside world more effectively than is possible for the prematurely born or fetal infant.

¼ Even the full-term neonate needs time to recover from the effects of the birth experience. Consequently, he is more or less dormant during the first day or two, or longer. His lack of adjustment to his new environment may show itself in fitful wakings, choking, irregular respiration, sneezing, regurgitations, and similar symptoms of instability.

Physical Characteristics. Postural changes from fetal confinement to infant relaxation of trunk and limbs may take several days. Immediately after birth there is a 6 to 9 per cent weight loss which may be caused by the loss of loosely stored water. The weight usually is regained within a week or ten days. Other symptoms of disorder that may be exhibited soon after birth normally begin to disappear by the fourth day. The neonate is now ready to go about his business of growing and developing, which usually proceeds rapidly in all areas.

Sensory Acuity. At or soon after birth, the infant gives evidence of the possession of elementary sensory functions. During the first two weeks, he may respond to light by turning his head in its direction. Startle (body jerk) and the closing of the eyelids can be induced by the sudden flashing of a bright light in front of his eyes. By the third week, he is able to follow moving objects with his eyes, which by this time are co-ordinated; at birth the eyes tend to move independently of each other.

Although it has been observed that some neonates respond to a loud noise by jumping or crying shortly after birth, this kind of response is relatively rare. Definite and consistent responses to sound are not common until the end of the second week or later, and then the sound needs to be fairly loud.

During the neonatal period, taste does not seem to be differentiated except for responses to sweet, salty, or bitter substances. Sensitivity to pain-producing stimuli appears to be somewhat developed at birth but increases during the first two weeks. Cold may arouse discomfort, but little is known concerning the infant's responses to other sensory stimulations.

The Reflexes. A healthy neonate gives evidence of certain well-functioning reflexes. These have begun to function during the fetal period, immediately at birth, or during the first few days of life. The pupillary reflex and turning the head toward a tap on the cheek may occur on the first day.

Rooted in prenatal activity are the Babinski and the Moro-embrace reflexes. The Babinski reflex is the extension of the big toe (often accompanied by the fanning of the toes) when the sole of the foot is stroked gently. The Moro reflex is a response to situations such as a sudden sound or the striking of a blow on the table or mattress upon which the infant is lying. His body jerks and he throws out his arms in a kind of embrace movement. These reflexes appear early in the neonatal period. They seem to disappear by the fourth month but are believed by some psychologists to be beginnings of later, more complex patterns of body response.

Of particular interest is the Darwinian or palmar reflex that can be found among children at birth. During the first few months, some children are able to support the weight of their bodies by grasping a rod extended to them. This appears to be a completely reflex action without cerebral control, and involves the utilization of the palm and fingers only. The presence of this reflex in the neonate has given rise to some unscientific but interesting speculation as to the possibility of its reflecting a primitive stage of human existence inherited from our ape and arboreal ancestors.

Certain other forms of behavior that appear at birth or soon thereafter would seem to be a part of an individual's native self-preserving equipment. These include sneezing, yawning, crying, hiccoughing, smiling, and sucking. Since these responses appear before the child has had an opportunity to learn them and their values to himself, they can be included among prenatally developed reflexes.

Other motor activities which do not properly come under the classification of reflexes are characteristic of infant behavior. The neonate tends to lie on his back with averted head. Usually, the arm on the side toward which his head is turned is extended and the other arm flexed toward the head-chest region. This general position is referred to as the *tonic-neck-reflex* attitude (t.n.r.). By the time the child is four weeks old, he may assume a startle position, in which his head centers and his legs and arms extend. He may also lash the air with his arms. Until he is about sixteen weeks old, however, the t.n.r. is his characteristic position.

Emotional and Social Responses. The so-called emotional reactions of the very young child are diffuse and therefore difficult to classify. Some psychologists claim that it is possible to differentiate infant behavior that expresses anger, fear, and love respectively. Whether one accepts this theory or not, it can be observed that in certain circumstances the neonate exhibits behavior that approximates what for the older child or adult may express one or another emotional state. For example, if the extremities of the infant are held down, he may begin to struggle against the bonds as if he were exhibiting rage. If he is held in the arms a short distance above a pillow and the arms are gently removed, he may start to cry and lash out with his arms as though to seek support — an apparent fear reaction. A pain-free infant who has just been fed is likely to coo, gurgle, smile, and snuggle into the arms of his mother or nurse as though he were trying to express feelings of affection. The neonate does give expression to moods, but the extent to which these differ from the reactions of other forms of animal life has not yet been satisfactorily determined.

By the end of the neonatal period, the child gives some slight evidence of the relation that exists between him and other persons. If he gives signs of discomfort when he is lying down, he tends to become quiet if he is picked up. His facial expression may change slightly when he is approached. He may respond to the human voice with some form of articulation. In general, however, the neonate is not concerned with environmental factors, except insofar as the presence of favorable ones would seem to give him a kind of vague, satisfying feeling of security, and their absence to disturb him.

Fond parents tend to watch every form of behavior exhibited by the very young child, and then attempt prejudiced interpretations of his behavior. This parental attitude is displayed particularly toward the first child.

MATURATION

There appears to be within each individual a strong urge to grow. This internal growth process of body organs and functions is called *maturation*. It means that specific body organs are ready to function at certain times and are not able to function until a minimum maturation has taken place. The walking of a child, for example, must await the maturation of his legs and other parts that coordinate walking movements; toilet training is not possible until the child has an awareness of a fullness of his bladder and the rectum through the maturation of the nerves that connect with these parts; learning to read is not achieved until the child develops his nervous system for language capacity, eye control, ability to concentrate, and the like.

After conception the developing individual is affected by both nurture and maturation. These processes proceed in an interlocking fashion as the growth and development of the individual continues. Neither nurture nor maturation exerts a continuous and separate impact at any one time. Nature has provided for certain body organs and functions to undergo the maturation process at appropriate times during the growth journey from conception through birth to maturity.

Maturation is concerned with those changes over which the individual has little or no control, such as the anatomical, physiological, and chemical changes that occur during growth and development. Growth takes place in an environment in which nurture enables maturation to become fullblown, and in which maturation is required as the individual moves gradually toward maturity. Not only are the mass responses developing into differentiated behavior but the process of integration is also taking place.

Just as special body parts are unable to function until there is sufficient maturation or readiness, so is learning delayed until both the nerous system and personal interest become ready. There is evidence that until a child has developed some readiness to learn, it is futile to attempt to give training in those body parts that have not undergone maturation. A display of interest in an activity is a good index of readiness.

CHAPTER 2

Anatomical and Physiological Development

The child inherits a specific bodily mechanism that possesses various potentialities for growth and development. From birth to adulthood, his body experiences many changes that, barring accidents, can be expected eventually to fit the individual for healthy and successful living. During the process of maturation, what happens to his body depends not only upon his natural growth pattern but also upon the ways in which natural growth is affected (favorably or adversely) by environmental factors.

GENERAL FACTORS IN THE STUDY OF GROWTH

The child is first and foremost a physical being. His physical constitution is basic to the development of his attitudes and behavior. Hence, it is necessary to study the patterns of his physical growth in order to understand other areas of development.

Methods of Studying Physical Growth. Studies of physical growth are numerous, including many areas of research. Some of these are: morphology, physiology and biochemistry, clinical medicine and pathology, psychology, mental hygiene, psychiatry, and public health and hygiene. Among outstanding centers of research are those at Harvard and Yale. Every measurable aspect of physical maturation and development is being investigated.

In studies of physical growth, either the horizontal or the longitudinal approach can be employed. Earlier studies were almost completely confined to research with large numbers of children at specific stages of development. By means of horizontal or cross-sectional measurement, conclusions were arrived at concerning growth tendencies in relation to sex, nationality, or race. At present

13

more emphasis is placed upon the longitudinal approach. Through its utilization a progressive study, covering a period of years, can be made of an individual's growth and developmental pattern.

A combination of the horizontal and the longitudinal approaches affords data that make it possible to compare an individual with himself and with others during various stages of growth.

Effect of Environment upon Growth. The maturation process determines the rate and amount of growth or modification that is possible for any specific organism. Environmental influences either help or hinder growth. The extrinsic factors of the environment responsible for the kinds of modification that take place include: family health history, diet, heat, cold, light, economic status, and experiences that grow out of the culture in which the child is born and reared.

Growth Rhythm. In the normal child, growth is rhythmic. Each individual's rate and limits of physical growth are peculiar to himself, although there are general similarities among human beings. Shift in rhythm and changes in rate of growth are apparent during the various maturational periods. Although new rhythms may appear in each cycle of growth, these maintain a constant ratio during the cycle. Moreover, each area (skeleton, nervous, circulatory, and digestive systems, etc.) has its own pattern of maturing — its specific rate, time of starting, and limit of growth. In general, however, normal growth is harmonious; at any stage of development there is evidenced a pattern of physical integration.

ANATOMICAL GROWTH

Significant areas of anatomical growth include: the skeleton, height and weight, body proportions, and the teeth.

Skeletal Changes. During the fetal and neonatal periods, the skeletal structure of the new organism is mostly cartilaginous. The infant's 270 bones are small, pliable, and spongy, and are loosely connected. The child at thirteen or fourteen years has 350 bones which have become ossified or hardened as a result of the depositing in the cartilage of calcium phosphate and other minerals. the fontanels (soft spots of the skull) close sometime between the ages of about one and a half and two years.

As the child matures beyond puberty, some of the small bones fuse during ossification. Small bony masses (epiphyses) appear in the cartilage at the ends of the bones. By the time adulthood is

14

reached, the epiphyses have fused to the extent that the skeleton now contains 206 bones that have broadened and thickened during the process of ossification.

Individual differences show themselves in skeletal growth as in other areas, but maturation of the bony structure is believed to be quite regular. Sex differences follow about the same pattern as the one for other aspects of physical growth. There appears to be a significant relationship between ossification and nutrition. Healthful diet promotes skeletal growth.

Height and Weight. Growth in height and weight is continuous, but it differs in rate for different cycles. Infancy and adolescence represent periods of rapid growth. Growth is relatively slower during the in-between years of childhood. Wide variations can be found among children, however, so that average trends in height and weight are useful mainly as guides in the measurement of individual children. The ratio between the height and the weight of any one child is significant only to the extent that it gives some indication of his physical health status, or that it deviates so widely from the accepted norm that the child is disturbed by comparisons between himself and more "normal" children of his age group.

Average Height. The average length of the newborn boy is about 20.5 inches and of the girl about 20.3 inches. Boys are slightly taller than girls at birth and maintain a height advantage until about the age of ten. At this time the height of the two sexes is approximately equal. During the next three or four years, girls take the lead over boys, but the latter regain the height advantage in their middle teens and keep it from then on. There are, of course, exceptional cases of very short men and tall women. According to estimates of age progress, boys have attained 57 per cent of their future height by the age of four years, and girls of the same age level 60 per cent. Boys continue their growth in height to the age of eighteen or over; girls usually reach full adult stature at about the age of sixteen.

The child can be expected to gain about ten inches during the first year and approximately four or five during the second year. The years from two to six represent a period of continued rapid growth, but less rapid than during the two previous years. From six to twelve the rate of growth slows down. The child may gain no more than two to three inches during this period. Then the rate of height growth may take a sudden spurt and continue more or less rapidly until full growth is attained.

Average Weight. At birth, the average boy weighs about 7

15

pounds and 8 ounces, and the weight of the average girl is about 7 pounds. By the end of the first year the weight probably has tripled. The greatest relative gain occurs during the first five months, by which time the infant may have doubled his weight at birth. From the fifth month onward the rate of growth gradually decreases. During the second year, the gain is only about one-half pound per month. By the fifty year, the average child's weight ranges between about 38 and 43 pounds, and between 80 and 95 pounds by the twelfth year.

For the first nine or ten years, the boy tends to be heavier than the girl. With the onset of pubesence, which usually is earlier for girls than for boys, the girl tends to exceed the boy in weight. During the early years of adolescence the boy again begins to be heavier than the girl and continues his weight advantage throughout the growing years and into adulthood.

Body Proportions. The newborn child's head represents about one-fourth of his total body's length. By the time the individual reaches adulthood the head constitutes approximately one-tenth of the total body length. The most rapid growth of the head takes place during the first two years after birth. The rate of growth then begins to decrease gradually. At the age of five, the head is about 90 per cent of its adult size; by the age of ten the percentage has increased to 95, and by fifteen or sixteen years of age the head can be expected to have attained its full growth.

Since the pattern of body growth is from the head downward, the upper parts of the body reach their maximum growth more quickly than do the lower parts. The growth of the face follows a similar pattern. The upper portion achieves approximately its full growth by the age of six years; the lower portion continues to change through adolescence.

The relatively "top-heavy" appearance of the young child's head that is caused by his prominent forehead, broad flat nose, and receding chin is in striking contrast to the contours of the adult face that gradually has changed proportionately to a wider and higher forehead, a broader and longer nose, a slightly jutting chin, and fuller lips. The relative growth of the features may be uneven, so that for a time an adolescent's face may take on a queer appearance. Also, although there seems to be little differentiation between the faces of a boy and a girl baby, the woman's face usually has finer features and is less rugged than that of the man.

16

Body contours also change. The chubby body of the one-year-old gradually becomes slimmer. The short limbs of the neonate stretch out to the extent that in adulthood they represent about half of the entire length of the body.

During the earlier years of life, there is relatively little difference in body contour between the sexes. Male and female pubertal changes bring about accompanying contour differences. The boy's form now is characterized by broad shoulders, slender hips, and straight leg lines. The hips of the girl grow wider, her leg lines become curved, but her shoulders remain narrow.

Growth of Teeth. A normal individual goes through the experience of having two sets of teeth erupt during his lifetime. By the end of the prenatal period, all the first or "baby" teeth have been formed in the gums. Although there are rare instances of a child's being born with one or more erupted teeth, the teeth usually begin to cut through by the sixth month of postnatal life. The lower front teeth usually appear first. The one-year-old can be expected to have eight teeth. All the deciduous teeth (first teeth) should have erupted by the time the child is four years old.

The permanent teeth have been maturing while the roots of the deciduous teeth have been disappearing. The child's first permanent tooth, the "six-year molar," erupts at about the age of six. The complete set of thirty-two teeth can be expected to have erupted by the time the child is twelve or thirteen years old. If "wisdom" teeth develop, they usually erupt during later adolescence or early adulthood. Girls tend to get their second teeth earlier than do boys.

PHYSIOLOGICAL DEVELOPMENT

No sharp differentiation can be made between the growth of body structure and the development of the body organs. Anatomical growth and physiological development represent two interdependent and overlapping phases of the maturational process.

The Nervour System. The beginnings of the nervous system are found in the embryonic stages of prenatal life. By the end of the first six months the fetus possesses the twelve billion or more nerve cells which comprise the nervous system. Some of these nerve cells have started to function by that time. As the fetus grows, they organize themselves into reaction patterns, and by the time the fetus is ready for expulsion from the uterus of the mother, the structural developments are complete. The developmental stages in the functioning of the various aspects of the system constitute an area of study that is difficult, highly technical, and still in its preliminary state.

At birth, the child's nervous system that has grown as a composite unit is composed of three types of networks of neurons that are concerned with different functions, operating as a unit for the welfare of the individual. The autonomic or sympathetic neurons control the life-preserving bodily organs such as the gastrointestinal tract (including the walls of the blood vessels), the respiratory apparatus, the genitourinary system, the rectum and bladder, and the glands — both duct and ductless.

Sensory and motor neurons include a vast network of neurons that reach all parts of the body. The sensory neurons extend to the skin and mucous membrane and to the special sense organs. The motor neurons function within the musculature of the head, neck, trunk, and extremities.

The third network of neurons, the association neurons, are concerned especially with voluntary and imaginal forms of behavior. These neurons deal more directly with perception and association of ideas, memory, language, and ideation.

The Brain. During the embryonic period the brain at first consists of three minute swellings that appear at the front end of the neural tube. As gradual growth takes place during the prenatal period, differentiations of form and function occur that eventually produce the highly complex but well-systematized organ that constitutes the basis of the individual's mental activity.

The weight of the brain at birth is greater in proportion to total body weight than it will be at any later time. In spite of this fact, the brain of the newborn infant has not reached its complete development. Hence, it is not ready to function along with the nervous system as it will later. By the fifty year the weight of the child's brain is about 80 per cent of its maximum weight; by the ninth year the percentage increases to about 90 per cent. Maximum brain weight usually is attained at about the twentieth year. The actual number of neurons is fixed during the prenatal period, but the brain cells grow and develop until the individual reaches maturity. The weight of the brain increases from an average of about 350 grams at birth to something between 1200 and 1400 grams at the end of adolescence.

18

The simple behavior of the very young child is controlled by the lower brain centers and the spinal cord. Later, the nerve cells of the cortex of the cerebrum have developed to the extent that intricate relationships are built up among them, resulting in increased mental activity. The *infragranular* layer of the cortex, attaining about 80 per cent of its growth at birth, controls the various reflexes. The *granular* layer, attaining 75 per cent of its growth at birth, is concerned with the conduction of sense impressions. The *supragranular* layer, attaining no more than 50 per cent of its growth at birth, co-ordinates, inhibits, and organizes the internal interactions of the nervous system into patterns of memory, speech, imagery, symbolism, and volition.

The Heart and the Circulatory System. As compared with its weight at birth, an individual's heart weighs from four to five times as much at the age of six, about seven times as much at the age of twelve, and twelve times as much at adulthood. The heart grows slowly between the ages of four and ten, with the greatest lag, as compared to general body growth, during the seventh year. Another slowing-down period may occur during preadolescence and early adolescence.

Pulse rate is highest at birth, decreasing with age. The average basal pulse rate per minute, at birth, is 144 for girls and 130 for boys. During the growing-up period to about the age of thirteen, the relative difference between boys and girls varies with the stages of growth. At three years of age the pulse rate is 90 for girls and 95 for boys, but at nine years of age it is 80 for both sexes. Beginning at thirteen, however, the pulse rate for girls is 76, decreasing to 69 at twenty years of age; the pulse rate for boys is 73 at thirteen and 62 at twenty years of age.

The average systolic blood pressure for both sexes ranges from 70 to 75 during the first few months of life and increases to a range of 105 to 128 between the ages of fifteen and twenty. During early childhood there is little difference in blood pressure between the sexes; from about thirteen years onward, the blood pressure of boys is higher than that of girls.

The Respiratory System. At birth the lungs are small. The ratio between the growth of the head and that of the chest is about as follows: at two years of age, they are about the same; at fifteen, the ratio is about two to three; and by adulthood it is three to five. Although the size of the chest continues to increase through adolescence, its shape remains the same after the age of thirteen.

19

The increase in the volume and weight of the lungs is great during the early years of adolescence and continues at a lesser rate until adulthood. The growth of the lungs is accompanied by increased breathing capacity. Maximum development usually is reached by girls at the age of seventeen, and by boys two or three years later.

The Digestive System. The shape of the neonate's stomach is tubular, and its position in the body is transverse. The capacity of the stomach at birth is about one ounce, which increases to three ounces by the end of the first month. As the size and position of the stomach change, it can hold more food and it empties more slowly. As can be expected, not only are the stomach and intestines small during childhood, but also the lining of the digestive tract is delicate and the digestive juices are less in amount that later in life.

The Muscles. The weight of the newborn child's muscles constitutes about 23 per cent of the total body weight. By the time he attains the age of eight years, this percentage has increased to 27, indicating that the growth of muscle tissue is relatively slow during childhood. Growth is more rapid during adolescence. At fifteen, the muscles weight almost 33 per cent, and one year later about 44 per cent, of the total body weight.

The increase of muscle weight after puberty is accompanied by an increase of thickness and length. As a result of these changes, the muscles develop greater strength and firmness. Consequently, they gain in power. Studies seem to indicate that there is little or no difference in the rate of growth between the so-called fundamental or large muscles of the arms, legs, and trunk and the small or "accessory" muscles of the face and eyes and of the hands and feet.

The Endocrine Glands. The endocrine or ductless glands, which discharge their secretion (hormones) directly into the blood stream, exercise a potent effect upon development. Located in various parts of the body, they appear to maintain a delicate chemical balance within the organism. The glandular system is complex and interdependent.

These glands do not follow the same or even a similar pattern of maturation. The thyroid, pancreas, and pituitary glands begin to function during the fetal state. Others develop later. These differences seem to indicate that certain glands affect development during one stage more than during another.

The Thyroid Gland. An important gland lying in the fore part of the neck, the thyroid, secretes a hormone, thyroxin, which affects an individual's rate of basal metabolism. Normally, the thyroid functions in such a way that the metabolic process is favorable to desirable physical development and consequent behavior. If this gland is overactive, however, the individual may give evidence of abnormal tensions and added physical activity. This condition is referred to as hyperthyroidism. Underactivity of the thyroid (hypothyroidism) results in generally sluggish behavior. The growth condition of the thyroid is directly related to the amount of iodine consumed by the individual.

The Parathyroids. Four small glands attached to the thyroid gland, the parathyroids, seem to have some control of calcium metabolism, with a possible effect upon ossification.

The Pituitary Gland. In the adult, the pituitary gland is about the size of a pea. It has two lobes — the anterior lobe and the posterior lobe.

One of the secretions of the anterior lobe appears to regulate skeletal growth. The underfunctioning or overfunctioning of this lobe is related to dwarfism or giantism, respectively. Another hormone from the anterior lobe can activate the sex glands or gonads. Precocious sex development may result from overactivity of this hormone. Obversely, deficiency of this hormone may result in the delay or nonoccurrence of sexual maturation.

We do not yet know very much concerning the functions served by the hormones of the posterior lobe. One function may be related to the tonus of the smooth muscles that line the digestive tract. They also may influence to some extent the burning of fat and the storing of water in the tissues.

The Adrenal or Suprarenal Glands. The adrenals are situated over each kidney. During an emotionalized state such as anger, there is an increase in the amount of adrenin (a hormone of these glands) that is released into the blood stream. This then gives rise to greater rapidity of heartbeat and an increase in blood pressure. These effects combined with a greater supply of glycogen (sugar) from the liver appear to increase greatly an individual's physical strength.

The Sex Glands or Gonads. After puberty, the testes and ovaries secrete reproductive cells — sperm and ova. They also produce hormones that regulate the development of secondary sex characteristics such as growth of the beard and change of voice in boys, and breast development and menstruation in girls. For both sexes, bodily and facial contours change with the onset of puberty, and hair appears in the public areas and in the arm pits.

More specifically, the primary function of the testes is to produce sperm cells; of the ovaries to produce ova or egg cells. However, the testes of the male have *interstitial* cells that secrete hormones and the ovaries of the female secrete hormones through the *corpus luteum.* The hormones secreted by the interstitial cells of the male and by the corupus luteum cells of the female account for the secondary sex characteristics. Theelin, for example, is one of the sex hormones which stimulates the breasts and reproductive organs, and remains active until the menopause.

The testicles of the male and the ovaries of the female develop within the abdominal cavity before birth. The ovaries are retained in this abdominl cavity throughout life; during the seventh prenatal month the testicles may descend into the scrotal sac, but are more likely to be delayed until sometime after birth. The gonads show a slight rise in growth in infancy, thereafter slowing down until about the tenth year, after which a sharp rise occurs which continues throughout puberty.

Certain hormones such as the *androgens* and *estrogens* are excreted by both boys and girls into the urine at a relatively early age. The amount of the excretion is rather small and not significantly different for either sex during the early years. At the beginning of puberty, however, the male excretes extrogens at about the same rate as earlier, but the female excretes them at a much increased rate. The latter may have some relationship with the menarche (menstruation period). There is a rate change also in the excretion of androgens, although this rate difference is not so great as with the estrogens.

The Thymus and the Pineal Gland. The thymus lies above the heart, and the pineal gland near the brain. Both of these glands are active during childhood. With the beginning of adolescence they disappear or become much less active. Their function seems to be to inhibit sexual maturation during the early years of life.

CHAPTER 3

Development of Motor Abilities

Motor abilities can be described briefly as the various kinds of bodily movements that are made possible through the co-ordination of nerve and muscle activity. All-round development is dependent in great part upon the mastery by the individual of motor skills that will facilitate the fulfillment of his physical and psychological needs and assist him to avoid harmful experiences.

GENERAL CHARACTERISTICS OF MOTOR ABILITIES

Some psychologists divide motor activities into two major categories: (1) gross movements that necessitate the movements of all or much of the body, e.g., walking, running, jumping, throwing, swimming, and skating; (2) finer motor skills that require the co-ordination of smaller muscles, e.g., grasping, drawing, writing, sewing, and using tools.

General Pattern of Development. Motor development has its roots in maturation. The child seems to be born with certain potentialities of neural and muscular response. Except for the earliest mass movements, the *form* taken by any movement is, perhaps, more or less influenced by the environmental conditions that are present while the motor ability is developing. To the extent that the mastery of a simple or more complex motor skill is directed in any way by extrinsic factors, it can be said that learning is taking place. No amount of guidance, however, can stimulate the development of motor ability in any area unless the organism is so constituted that maturation, apart from learning, is possible.

The development of motor abilities appears to follow a more or less sequential pattern, especially during the early years. The bases of this pattern lie in the rate and kind of structural growth that is taking place.

Results of Research. Motor development was one of the earliest fields of scientific study. Begun in a systematic way by Galton in the nineteenth century, research into the development of motor ability continues to be a fertile area. One of the general conclusions that seems to have emerged from the many investigations is the fact that the trend of development in motor abilities is from general coordinated movement to many more specific kinds of motor behavior. This "mass to specific trend" has not yet been accepted as a general law, but experimental evidence appears to be in its favor.

The sequential pattern of growth from head downward is accepted as a general principle. By the "cephalocaudal trend" is meant that there is a more or less orderly progress from head to foot in the development of motor ability. It also has been concluded, as a result of research, that co-ordinated trunk or torso movements precede those of the body extremities. This sequence is referred to as the "proximodistal trend."

PRENATAL AND NEONATAL MOTOR DEVELOPMENT

The first movements of the neonate represent a continuation and differentiation of movements begun during the fetal period. The behavior responses of the fetus and of the newborn infant consist of two kinds — general mass activity and some specific movements.

Movements of the Fetus. The fetus begins to stir before the ninth week. It is believed that during the third month he is able to move his neck and trunk, rotate his rump, move his bent arms backwards, and extend his legs. These movements are feeble and show little coordination but signify the beginnings of motor abilities.

During the period of gestation that includes roughly the period between the twelfth and fourteenth weeks, the fetus displays various patterns of elementary movement. His earlier generalized movements take on a more specific character. Head movements occur independently of trunk movements. Within the confines of the amnion (membranous sac) the arms and legs become more mobile at the joints and fly out mildly into space. These reactions seem to be detached from one another. The head, the hands, and the feet go into action with no apparent relation among them, yet

24

their behavior represents a unitary growth plan. Elbows show mobility; hands move and can be opened and closed; feet are moved easily; the toes, especially the big toes, show great mobility.

From the sixteenth to the twentieth week the movements of the fetus can be recognized by the mother, first as slight flutterings but later as vigorous movements. During this period other more differentiated movements begin. The eyeballs already have begun to move. Now blinking of the eyes may begin. Protruding movements of the lips may start and the closing of the fist that occurred earlier now takes on the pattern of grasping.

By the twenty-fourth week the fetus has achieved certain patterns or mobility that are preparing him to begin, with birth, the development of his motor ability. Instead of occasional exhalation movements of the chest, the fetus now would be able to inspire and expire and to produce a thin crying sound if he were removed from the amnion to another environment.

Other movements that can be recognized by the mother are sudden jerks and kicks, and turning and squirming. Much of the probable differentiation of behavior that is taking place during the last month of the fetal period cannot be recognized. The organs are consolidating into an integrating pattern. It probably is safe to assume that the reactions that do take place are acquiring their specific life functions.

Neonatal Motor Development. At birth, the child is capable of varied, diffuse, and rapid movement. Stimulation of any part of the body appears to stimulate motor activity of the whole body, although exceptions to this general pattern can be found. Such seemingly localized activities as sneezing and crying stimulate mass activity. Even during the sleeping or quasi-dormant state in which the neonate spends most of his day, body movements are observable. According to certain investigations of infant behavior, there seems to be a relationship between the neonate's body condition and his mass activity. Greatest activity occurs when he is experiencing pain, hunger, or physical discomfort. A wide-awake, hungry infant, for example, is capable of about fifty movements per minute.

The specific activities of the very young infant include the reflexes and other general responses to stimuli. Necessary for survival are reflexes such as the pupillary reflex, digestion, breathing, sneezing, and heart action. Other general responses vary in their degree of aimlessness and lack of co-ordination, but they are basic to the later acquisition of skilled motor ability. Among the most common of these responses can be listed: feeding responses, spontaneous eye movements, trunk-turning movements, turning and lifting the head, hand and arm movements, and leg and foot movements.

SITTING UP AND WALKING

The development of the postural-locomotor abilities follows a relatively regular schedule for the average child. The exact date at which a certain stage of this development occurs is not nearly so important as some mothers seem to believe it is. There are individual differences in this area of growth and development as in all other aspects. Hence, any specific time referred to in this and subsequent discussions of motor development is approximate rather than exact and may vary considerably among some children.

Upright Posture. During the first weeks of postnatal life, the infant has little control over his body. The first controls are of the head and neck. By the time he is about four weeks old, he is able to lift his head when held to the shoulder of an adult or while he is in a prone position (lying with face down). At sixteen weeks he can raise his head, with the face almost perpendicularly upward, from a prone position, can rotate it from side to side when he is in a supine position (lying flat with face up), and can hold it erect if he is supported while sitting. By the time he is about six months old, the baby in a prone position can hold his head erect and rotate it while he is supporting himself on extended arms.

The eight-weeks-old baby can turn his body from side to side. This is followed by a turning from back to side (fourth month), and then by a complete turn from stomach to stomach (sixth month). During this process, the back, which up to twelve weeks is rounded, begins to straighten. Since growth, in general, is from the head downwards, the upper part of the back straightens first. At thirty-six weeks, the back is held erect for an indefinite length of time.

By the time the baby is nine or ten months old he can sit without support. He is now halfway between the supine position and walking. At first he needs to be helped to attain the sitting position.

Walking. The baby soon learns to change from a prone to a sitting position and then back to the prone position. By this time he is likely to begin to crawl, and then to creep toward an object that attracts his attention. He may vary the activity by scooting or

26

hitching. Objects of interest beyond his sitting or creeping reach now stimulate the child to pull himself up to a standing position. At first he may need help, not only to get himself up but also to get back to a prone position. After he has mastered the ability to stand unsupported, he may attempt to take a few steps holding on to a support. Gradually, he begins to walk, falteringly at first and then with increasing confidence.

The rate at which children develop the power to walk varies widely. Physical defects, ill health, excessive weight, or other abnormal conditions may delay what might be considered a normal pattern of development.

With the mastery of walking on an even surface, the child branches out in his activities. During the second year, he learns to walk up and down stairs, to run, to walk sideways and backward, and to climb up on furniture. The third year brings ability to jump with both feet together, to gallop, to jump down from low objects, and to turn somersaults. The child improves these abilities during the fourth year. By the fifth year he has mastered all or most of the fundamental forms of locomotion, some of them to a high degree of skill.

DEVELOPMENT OF ARM AND HAND ABILITY

The arm lashings and the more or less aimless, reflex grasping or prehensile movements of the hand exhibited during the neonatal period are precursors of the many skilled manual activities in which the individual probably will engage by the time he reaches maturity. As in the case of the development of walking, the development of arm-hand control appears to follow a more or less regular pattern. Here again, individual differences are manifested. The acquisition of manual skill is dependent upon sensory acuity, especially tactual, visual, and kinesthetic.

Development of Prehension. The grasping reflex of the infant is digital; by the fifth month there is some use of the thumb, and by the ninth month palmar grasping (or grasping with the thumb in opposition to the forefinger) has been developed. The palmar grasp is characteristic of most of the prehension of the individual through adulthood.

During early infancy there is no co-ordination between the eye and the hand. Investigators have found that the ability to follow a moving object with the eyes through an arc of about 90 degrees is developed by the fourth week; at twelve weeks, the length of the arc is extended to 180 degrees. During this period the child makes no attempt to touch an object, such as a cube, that is placed before him. By the age of forty weeks a child can be expected to have developed sufficient eye-hand co-ordination to see and touch cube placed before him.

The first attempt by a child to reach for a cube may be a "backhand" approach. The "circuitous" approach is used most frequently and the "straight" approach shows the greatest maturity. Body posture in reaching also changes. At first the reaching is dominated by the shoulder; after that, in sequential order, by the elbow, the fingers, and the wrist. When the child is about a year old, he makes a straight approach in reaching, and the arm is controlled and aimed at the object by the wrist and forefinger. Complete development of reaching movements is not attained, however, until the child is four or five years old.

Accompanying the child's learning to reach for an object is the development of his ability to grasp it. At sixteen weeks, the child may reach and stare at a cube for about five seconds but does not attempt to grasp it. The twenty-week-old pulls the cube toward his body or other hand. This movement is referred to as the "squeeze grasp." From then on the baby appears to be experimenting with various types of grasp. All of them are awkward and unsatisfying until, by the time he is about one year old, he has developed the ability to grip the cube between the fingers and thumb (called the "pincer movement") and hold it without resting his arm on a table.

During this period the child engages in other manipulatory movements. He first puts his hand on the bottle while feeding and later pats it, and picks up small objects within his reach, which he attempts to put into his mouth. At the end of the first year, he may be able to hold a cup and even to experiment with a spoon. A year later he can pour milk from a small pitcher into a cup and manipulate a fork. By the time that he is five years old he can talk and eat at the same time, attempt to cut his meat with a knife, and help in the clearing of the table, the dusting of the legs of tables and chairs, and other simple household chores.

The play movements of the child exhibit a similar pattern of improvement. Beginning at about twenty-four weeks with the grasping of a rattle, the child learns by the end of the year to reach for play toys with both hands. A little later he is able to play ball with another person who is standing not too far removed from him. Play activities involving arm and hand manipulation are fairly well developed by the sixth year.

Writing Movements. Before the age of three years the child passes through progressive stages as follows: holds a crayon in his hand (mostly by shoulder movements) by seven months, draws the point of it across the paper at eighteen months, and begins to scribble between the ages of two and three years. By the time he is in his fourth year, he probably can manipulate a soft pencil instead of a crayon, has improved his grip, and can draw simple representations of things in his environment, such as a house or a man. During this stage he also develops the ability to trace.

The sixth year usually finds the child able to exercise considerable control of the writing implement. He tends to write with the wrist and fingers, and his writing shows greater ease and regularity. By the twelfth year the child can be expected to have developed his own individual style of writing in terms of his training.

Handedness. The one-year-old child may appear to "favor" one hand over the other in reaching for objects, but specific hand preference usually is not definite until the third or fourth year. For most children the preferred hand is the right hand. Left-handedness is relatively uncommon but has led to much controversy concerning its possible causes and the most appropriate attitude to be developed toward it.

During the first year of life, at least, there appears to be neither complete left- nor right-handedness. As the child matures, he begins to show eye, hand, and foot preferences, but these do not always exhibit a definite uniformity. Evidences of ambidexterity are found even among adults, depending upon the activity engaged in.

Since the child develops in a right-handed world it is likely that he will become right-handed, as he imitates the hand preference of those about him. If he seems to prefer the left hand, it probably would not hurt him to be encouraged to change to the right, if the conditioning is started early. In cases where left-handedness appears to persist, the best procedure for the adult to follow is that of doing nothing about it, allowing the child to pursue his natural pattern of development.

DEVELOPMENT OF SPECIFIC MOTOR SKILLS

The three-year-old child can be expected to have developed a fair degree of gross muscular control. The six-year-old has mastered many of the fundamental motor abilities that are needed for survival. He can walk, run and jump, feed himself, put on and remove his clothing, assist with simple household tasks, communicate orally with others, and participate in many play activities that necessitate the co-operation of the sense organs and many body muscles.

From the age of six onward, two types of development are in progress: the improvement of the basic abilities and the learning of finer, more complex motor skills. In both fundamental and more specific motor activity, the development of abilities centers around the improvement of precision and accuracy, speed, steadiness, and strength of voluntary movements.

There are many factors which influence the degree to which one or another motor ability is perfected or delayed in its utilization. These factors include environmental influences and opportunities to practice a skill, physical size, health condition, nutrition, mental status, and the extent to which fear has been produced by earlier unsuccessful attempts to perform. Adult attitudes may also affect an individual's ability to perfect a motor skill. For example, boys generally excel girls in most physical activities, such as jumping, running, basketball-throwing, and similar physical activities. One reason for this probably is rooted in physical constitution; however, in the past, if not at present, girls have been discouraged from participation to any great extent in these sports as they were considered to be "unladylike."

The development of specific motor skills probably does not lend itself to such detailed and progressive study as do the earlier grossest movements. Motor tests have been devised, however, to measure the extent to which, at any given period of learning a motor skill, a child has improved in speed, precision, steadiness, or general accomplishment.

Studies dealing with motor progress during childhood have yielded sufficiently valid results to warrant the acceptance of certain principles of development. Some of these principles are:

1. Speed of voluntary movement improves at a fairly uniform rate during childhood.

2. Accuracy of voluntary movement shows rapid improvement during the preschool and elementary school periods.

3. According to some psychologists, steadiness in motor behavior continues to improve throughout the childhood years.

4. Since relative strength can be affected by one or more environmental conditions, progress in this respect is variable.

5. Except in the early years, there appears to be little correlation between intellectual ability and certain types of motor performance.

6. Rapid improvement in complex motor skills is generally characteristic of adolescent years.

Tests of motor skills are specific to the respective situations in which they are used. Moreover, skill in a mechanical ability is dependent on other factors besides motor ability as such. For these reasons, tests of motor skills constructed to date do not yield completely satisfying information, although their results indicate definite trends characteristic of motor development in the more or less typical individual.

Speed and Accuracy in Motor Learning. Whether to emphasize speed at the expense of accuracy continues to confront persons who give instruction in certain motor skills. Both speed and accuracy are important in the learning of such motor responses as eye-movements in reading, learning to type, learning to play a musical instrument, or mastering a variety of motor activities. Experience has shown that both speed and accuracy should be considered together from the start of training. For example, skill in typing is best acquired when consideration is given simultaneously to both speed and accuracy.

When speed and accuracy are emphasized by the teacher, the child strives to attain these twin goals. Accuracy should not be sacrificed for speed; yet slow performance does not guarantee accuracy. Beginners should be encouraged to complete the motor patterns at an acceptable speed, regardless of the errors that may be made. Practice of these complete patterns should continue as the individual attempts to eliminate any errors, until definite progress has been achieved. Emphasis should be placed on careful and painstaking execution that leads to the achievement of near perfect results. Hence motor learning should begin with learning by "whole" responses in which attention is given to both speed and accuracy. Yet, part learning may be needed to refine those weaknesses that have been discovered during the complete performance.

CHAPTER 4

Development of the Art of Intercommunication

The art of intercommunication, commonly referred to as the *language arts,* includes sensory responses, such as looking and listening, and sensory-motor reactions, particularly speaking, writing, and drawing. Implicit in the achievement of satisfactory intercommunication are the abilities to understand the gestures and facial expressions of another person and his oral and written forms of language, as well as the ability to develop understandable communication patterns of one's own. The growth of the art of intercommunication follows a course from birth onward that is relatively similar to progress in other aspects of development and closely interrelated with them.

BEGINNINGS OF INTERCOMMUNICATION

If a child is normal at birth he possesses all the potentialities needed for the gradual development of the various forms of inter-communication. Some writers divide the progressive stages of language development according to the following general categories: (1) reflex sounds and feeble festures, (2) babbling, (3) use of simple words, (4) more or less meaningful one-word sentences, (5) the combination of words into thought units — oral and written, (6) mastery of the language arts.

The progress of the development of language ability generally is continuous. There is no sharp difference between the end of one period and the beginning of the next, although the rates of progress may vary from time to time. There also is some overlapping of sequential patterns.

THE DEVELOPMENT OF SPEECH PATTERNS

From the beginning of its development, language has social significance. From the earliest years onward, an individual uses one or another form of language to indicate his wants and needs. The earliest forms of expression are overt. As the child progresses in his power to adapt his behavior to the interests and wishes of others, he gradually learns to suppress his impulse to "talk out loud." His speech becomes subvocal and then, for the most part, silent speech (thinking).

Stages in Speech Progress. Investigators differ as to whether the birth cry constitutes the first attempt at communication or should be regarded merely as a reflex. It is generally agreed, however, that the infant's gestures and first vocalizations may be indications of his needs and wants. Crying, accompanied by body movement, becomes differentiated by the end of the third week, in terms of hunger, cold, pain, wetness, and other physiological states. As the infant grows, his crying becomes more specific to the situation by which he is conditioned.

During the first few months, the child also gives expression to many different kinds of explosive vocalizations, in which some investigators find the beginnings of basic speech sound. These sounds, commonly referred to as *cooing,* are unlearned, resulting from chance movements of the vocal organs. At first these vocalizations resemble vowel sounds more than they do consonants.

Babbling. The babbling stage usually extends from the third to the eighth month. This represents a gradual development of the sounds made earlier. The child apparently selects (without any reasoning) those sounds which give him pleasure and continues to repeat them for his own satisfaction and probably for the delight of his parents who encourage him in this practice. Consequently, he may iterate many times and with some slight rhythm and inflection such meaningless expressions as *da-da, ma-ma, oddle-oddle, uggle-uggle.* Too often, adults try to put meaning into these random vocalizations, especially *da-da* and *ma-ma.*

Gestures. As a substitute for intelligible speech the young child soon becomes proficient in the use of gestures and whole-body movement. A baby who does not want any more food may push the nipple away from his mouth, turn his head away from the nipple, pucker up his face, or close his lips. He may wiggle and squirm when he is held and wants to be free. He will hold out his arms and smile if he wants to be picked up from his crib and be held.

As the child learns to be articulate in the vocal expression of his wishes, he is less dependent upon gestures. As he matures, hand gestures, facial grimaces, and other gestures are employed for the purpose of emphasizing the spoken word. For the most part, these represent imitation of behavior habits observed in associates.

Development of Word Usage. In order to give expression to his wants, interests, and thoughts, the child must achieve mastery of four aspects of intercommunication through speech: understanding what others say, developing a vocabulary of his own, learning to pronounce words correctly, and achieving acceptable sentence structure.

Word Usage. Even the very young child appears to understand the significance in relation to himself of certain simple words or combinations of words such as "No!" or "No, no," "Shake bye-bye," and similar suggestive terms used by parents and other adults. Since the spoken word or phrase usually is accompanied by an appropriate gesture and facial expression, it is difficult to determine whether the baby is responding to the spoken word or to the total situation. It is probably true, however, that he comprehends much of what is said to him before he can express himself in words.

As the child learns to understand the meaning of words and sentences he begins to build his vocabulary. At first, this may consist of no more than the imitative repetition of words he hears, with little or no understanding of their connotation. He gradually develops a vocabulary that is useful to him. His first words are nouns that are employed by him in a general sense. All men are "daddy." Women are "mamma." The term "doggy" is applied to any kind of dog and may have different implications such as "See the doggy," "I want the doggy," or "I pat the doggy." This use of the noun only to express action of one kind or another is referred to by some psychologists as the *word sentence.* Later, the child may use simple action verbs; still later, simple adjectives find their way into his speech pattern.

The child appears to be sparing in his use of words to express his wants or feelings. At first, he also use his name or the word "baby" in place of a pronoun. For example, "Baby eat" or "I am hungry"; "Johnny go choo-choo" is the young child's way of

34

saying "I want a train ride." Emotional states find expression in such forms as "Good baby," "Bad mamma," and the like. These verbal expressions usually are accompanied by appropriate gestures.

Vocabulary. By the time he is eighteen months old, the child may be expected to have achieved an average of about ten or twelve simple words, although the range may extend from three or four to one hundred. His vocabulary increases rapidly during the next three or four months.

From about two to two and one-half years of age the child possesses a vocabulary of from two hundred to three hundred words, although some studies indicate that a few children can give evidence of vocabularies extending into the thousands. The three-year-old probably has acquired a vocabulary of a thousand words or more, which continues to increase. Recent studies in the field credit him at the age of twelve with a recognition vocabulary well in excess of thirty thousand words and a usage vocabulary somewhere in the neighborhood of ten thousand words.

Verbal Language. Beginning with the one- or two-word phrase, the child rapidly achieves the ability to pattern his sentence structure upon the models by which he is stimulated. From the age of two or thereabouts throughout childhood he gradually progresses toward a relatively adult pattern of oral expression.

Age Period — Two to Three. Although the one- or two-word sentence can still be heard, the child is beginning to use longer sentences and to vary their form. A few examples are: "Cup all gone," "I see daddy go bye-bye car," "I like weet tatoes (sweet potatoes)." Another sign of progress during this stage of development is the increased use of pronouns, especially *I, me,* and *you.* The child does not always use the first two correctly, e.g., "Me want to go." Toward the end of this period there also may be evidenced the correct use of plurals and of past tense. The sentence structure of the three-year-old tends to become more complex. Parts of speech, mood, and tense are recognized, although they still may be used inadequately. The "talking stage" may have begun.

Age Period — Four to Five. Sentence structure has improved by the fourth year. The child likewise becomes more and more sentive to correct grammatical usage. He becomes extremely talkative, not only with others but to himself. He appears to show interest and concern about matters not connected with the present situation, and he evinces interest in others besides himself. He asks many questions, sometimes not waiting for an answer to one before asking another. He seems to be intrigued by his developing powers of expression and to be eager to practice his newly found ability.

The child of kindergarten age displays a fairly efficient control of oral expression. He still lacks understanding of many of the accepted niceties of word meaning, pronunciation, and grammatical usage. This can come only through training, and sometimes is not mastered by adults.

Later Childhood. By the time the child enters elementary school he probably has developed a relatively fair appreciation of the language standards to be applied and the limitations to be observed as set by adult society. He is ready to use speech as a means of relatively intelligent intercommunication and as a tool for learning.

The child's school and other social experiences are potent factors in the development of his verbal speech patterns. The length and complexity of his sentences gradually increase. The preadolescent can talk fluently about many kinds of topics, without always understanding, however, the import of what he is saying. His grammatical structure (when he is careful) usually is satisfactory. He is sensitive to correct pronunciation and tends to enunciate with precision and clarity.

Factors of Speech Development. Although the development of the speech pattern can be expected to follow certain more or less uniform cycles, various factors either help or hinder progress at the different age levels. The most common of these influences are: general growth rate, intelligence, sex, and socioeconomic status. Bilingualism in the family also may have an effect upon a child's rate and kind of speech development.

General Growth Rate. Some children display a physical and psychological maturation pattern that is either more rapid or slower than what can be considered average or normal. Studies have shown that in cases of children whose general growth sequence was "ahead" of itself, the speech mechanisms were so far advanced in their development that the early stages of vocalization appeared to be telescoped. The young child was able to make distinguishable sounds and put meaning into them long before this normally could be expected.

Contrariwise, parents sometimes are disturbed by the fact that their child does not "learn to talk" so early or so rapidly as do other children in the same family or in neighbors' families. In such cases, the difficulty may be caused by a generally slow process of

36

growth. Given time, without being forced, the child probably will catch up with his peers by the time he is six or seven and then possibly outstrip them in his ability to speak. If, however, retarded speech is an accompaniment of retarded or deficient mental development the child may continue to have difficulty in achievnig satisfactory powers of intercommunication.

Intelligence. A child's degree of mental alertness at any stage of his development would seem to exercise a potent influence upon the degree of facility with which and the rate at which he achieves intelligible speech and acceptable speech patterns. The bright child may begin to talk as much as four months earlier than the so-called average child. The mentally slow child may be delayed three years in his development of an acceptable speech pattern. Feeble-minded children show great variation in the extent to which they ever develop intelligible speech.

The mentally alert child not only begins to speak early but also appears to be quick in developing a mature pattern of speech. This facility sometimes causes adults to expect of him a kind of adult power of thinking that is beyond him. In this connection, it also has been found that some children display a precocity in their early speech behavior that is not continued. By the time they are ready for elementary school or later, their reactions seem to have slowed down to a point where they are no better than a good average. The opposite also is true. A slow beginner may seem to take a sudden spurt during his elementary school days and excel the supposedly normal children of his age and school group. This is an experience common to teachers who have taught the same children in the first grade and then again in a higher grade.

Sex. According to studies in this field it seems that, in general, girls begin to speak earlier than boys do, and use longer sentences earlier. Girls excel in their development of general speech patterns, such as length of sentence, grammatical correctness, word usage, comprehensibility, and loquacity. On the average, girls appear to develop a larger vocabulary than do boys and to achieve it earlier. This superiority, although slight in some instances, continues to maturity. Some boys, however, may finally exceed girls in their maximum development of speech patterns.

Socioeconomic Status. It is generally agreed that children reared in homes reflecting a favorable socioeconomic status are superior in language ability to children who come from homes of lower status. Some psychologists claim that there may be as much as eight months' difference in the rate of development. It also has been observed that school entrants who come from "better" homes seem to have developed by that time a better speech pattern, a larger vocabulary, and greater loquacity than have children who are the products of "poorer" homes or of institutions.

There is not so general an agreement concerning the causes of these differences. Adults who have been able to achieve an adequate socioeconomic status are assumed to possess a relatively high intelligence status and a superior educational background. Hence, it can be expected that a child of such parents will have inherited good mental ability and, during his growing years, will have been surrounded by relatively acceptable speech patterns. Since much of the child's vocabulary and general speech pattern are acquired through imitation, it would seem logical to conclude that good biological inheritance plus favorable environmental conditions tend to result in superior language development.

Other Factors. A factor that is not related to the socioeconomic status, but is associated with the home, is the effect of multiple births. Twins, triplets, or other multiple-birth children appear to be slower in their early speech development than is a singleton. They seem to develop a jargon used between or among themselves and to meet their early childhood needs without too much dependence upon intelligible speech. This situation becomes modified considerably when these children go to school.

Another factor that may affect a child's rate and kind of language development is the extent to which he may be exposed to a second language in the home, especially during the early formative years. A child of foreign parents may experience confusion, not only of vocabulary but also of pronunciation and idiom.

The extent to which encironmental factors affect native endowment can be determined to some extent by the progress made by the child as a result of school learning and classroom environment. Even on the school level, however, the continued effects upon him of home influence and the influences of close associates may accelerate or retard his progress.

Speech Difficulties. From the lower schools through the college level, considerable attention is being focused upon speech improvement. Speech difficulties may range from "sloppy" speech, resulting mainly from inadequate or faulty learning, to actual speech disorders that have their roots in organic conditions or emotional tensions.

38

Faulty Speech. As a result of inadequate learning or slow maturation during babyhood and the preschool years, a child may develop unintelligible speech or incorrect speech patterns. There are several common types of faulty speech. Essential letters, syllables, or words may be omitted, e.g., *thow* for *throw,* or *milk good* for *the milk is good.* The incorrect verb, pronoun, or preposition may be used; letters may be interchanged in a word or syllable. Errors such as these constitute what is generally referred to as *"baby" talk.* If these incorrect speech patterns are encouraged as "cute" or imitated by adults in their conversations with young children, the habit patterns tend to persist well into later childhood. Certain ungrammatical forms continue through adulthood if they are not checked early. Notable among these are the double negative and the incorrect use of certain pronouns, especially *I* and *me,* and *who* and *whom.* In general, however, these early childhood errors respond successfully to patient and consistent correction.

Speech Disorders. Speech defects or disorders that tend to persist or that appear later in the child's life are much more serious than the faulty speech of the young child. Some of these defects require surgical attention; some respond more or less favorably to other forms of therapy. It appears that speech defects are more common among boys than among girls. Some of the serious defects are intensified forms of early faulty speech patterns.

Speech disorders may take any one of various forms of difficulties or combinations of them. The "hissing *s*", often caused by spaces between the front teeth, may be combined with "lateral emission," associated with incorrect control of air while speaking. A few of the more common forms of serious speech disorders are: lisping, slurring, stuttering, and stammering.

Lisping. The substitution of letter sounds, e.g., *tith* for *this,* may be an uncorrected continuation of "baby" talk. Such cases respond easily to training unless the habit has become fixed. The defect is more serious if it results from a deformity of the jaw, lips, or teeth. Unless the physical difficulty can be corrected, the child must be helped to develop new patterns of letter formation.

Slurring. Slurring, or the running of words together in such way as to cause unintelligible speech, may result from any one of various conditions. Sometimes the child, especially as a school entrant, is so eager to talk that he appears to be "tumbling all over himself" in his attempts to say all that he wants to say. Consequently, his speech is rapid and his words are enunciated indistinctly. A child who has developed his speech patterns in the relatively secluded environment of the home may become "tongue-tied" in the presence of strangers. His fear of these alien influences results either in his apparent inability to talk at all or in the mumbling of words through partially closed lips. Most serious is the slurring that is caused by organic difficulties such as lack of tongue development, paralysis of the vocal organs, or difficulties of the lips or jaw.

Stuttering and Stammering. Both of these speech difficulties seem to have their roots in emotional tensions or in other forms of emotional maladjustment. Fear of failure, a feeling of insecurity in a particular situation, or attempted speech improvement resulting from overprodding by adults are among the factors that may give rise to one or both of these disorders.

Some studies have shown a possible hereditary base. At one time it was believed that the development of stuttering was associated with attempts to change a child's hand preference from left to right. This theory is not generally accepted at present. Whatever evidence there may be of a displayed association between the two can be explained in terms of emotional tensions experienced by a child as he attempts to respond to adult pressures exerted upon him to change hand habits already developed.

Although stuttering and stammering often are linked to each other, there is a behavioral difference between them. In stuttering the individual tends to repeat sounds, words, or phrases. He often has difficulty in enunciating the first consonant letter of a word, as *d-d-drink.*

The stammerer seems to be unable to produce any speech sound. He gasps, hesitates, gasps again, and mouths the word. He finally may be able to produce it. Since facial grimaces and other spasmodic movements may accompany the individual's attempts to articulate promptly and effectively, the embarrassment caused him by the effect of his struggles on his associates may intensify his nervous and emotional tension. If no organic difficulty is apparent, therapy needs to be applied that will relax the patient's emotional tonus. Patience on the part of both the therapist and the client are needed if the condition is to ameliorated or overcome.

DEVELOPMENT OF READING ABILITY

The development of reading ability is closely related to other aspects of growth and development, especially speech development. Also, as is true of speech development, girls excel boys in reading readiness by the time they reach schoolage.

Before the Age of Three. The young child's reading experiences are limited to the more or less accurate identification of simple, detail-free pictures. At the age of about eighteen months the child can point to pictures in a book that previously have been identified. He then may learn to say, for example, "bow-wow" when shown a picture of a dog. By the time he is two years old he should be able to name pictures of objects, animals, or people with which he has had experience. During the next year he develops the ability to name certain letters on blocks or in alphabet books.

Ages Four and Five. By the time a child reaches his fourth year, he usually has acquired the ability to recognize his first name and identify word signs such as *hot* and *cold* on faucets, or *stop* and *go*. He also may be able to read letters in sequence and ask what they spell. The child of this age is beginning to gain a little understanding of word symbols. Toward the end of this period he likes to listen to a story that is being read to him while he looks at both the pictures and the text.

Later Development. When the child enters the elementary school at the age of six he can be expected to differentiate between small and capital letters, and to recognize words and word combinations. He can match words and find specific words that relate to a story being read to him. He also may seem to be able to read simple stories that at one time were repeated by him from memory. His general attitude now is one of interest in words in relation to himself and to his experiences.

Beginning with the seventh year, the child starts to read on his own. Although he may make mistakes or omit words or syllables, he shows some mastery of the printed page. He begins to spell words that are a little more difficult than the *cat* and *dog* level, the spelling of which may have developed earlier with parental encouragement. He likes to read aloud. In his eagerness to finish a sentence, he may omit words. It is not always evident that he understands what he is reading. During this year he also begins to read silently. Some children seem to prefer silent reading to oral reading.

With the ninth year begins the child's interest in reading stories related to materials and events outside his own experiences. He may want to read about all kinds of different places and things. His silent reading shows improvement, since he is able to put more meaning into the printed page. His oral reading may still be more or less mechanical, but memory for facts seems to respond better to oral than to silent reading. The average child's reading progress from now on is closely related to the kind of training he receives and the amount of encouragement to read he experiences, both in the home and at school.

Factors of Reading Development. The child's rate and achieved efficiency in reading is dependent upon various factors. There are great individual differences among children in this aspect of development. Visual and auditory acuity, mental ability, and environmental conditions exercise a potent influence upon reading progress.

The emotionalized attitudes of the child also must be considered. If he appears to be a little slower than others during his early school experiences in reading, he may lose confidence in himself and develop a fear and dislike of reading situations. On the other hand, the quick young reader is thereby helped to develop self-assurance, and is stimulated toward further reading progress. He usually is the child who can be found browsing in a library for books that might seem to be beyond his age and maturity level.

DEVELOPMENT OF WRITTEN EXPRESSION

In order to develop the ability to communicate with others by means of the written word, the child must have acquired adequate penmanship skill and an adequate usage vocabulary, i.e., words which he can spell and of which he understands the meaning. He also must have achieved the power to arrange words in simple sentence form, with some knowledge of capitalization. Most important of all, probably, is the felt need to engage in one or another form of written communication. Since modern children seem to learn early to communicate with their friends by telephone, former stimuli, such as inviting friends to a party or accepting invitations, no longer have the potency that they once had.

When the child enters school or in some cases during preschool years he is encouraged to express his thoughts, interests, and feelings in written form. This activity poses many problems: to have something to say, to find the right words in which to say it and to spell these words correctly, to express one's thoughts in

42

acceptable form, and to write legibly with proper attention to such mechanics as space relationships, margins, and general neatness of appearance. Each of these skills must be mastered by the child before he can be said to have developed adequately the art of written communication.

Acquiring Skill in Penmanship. Young children are in the age at which they begin to "scribble" with crayon or chalk. At first, muscular control is lacking, but indiscriminate markings gradually come to be forms that have meaning for the child. By the age of five, he usually has developed some manipulative control and a recognition of the association between vision and kinesthetic sensations. He uses free arm movements, often accompanied by facial grimaces, and his scriblings are large, covering the entire page. Later he is able to imitate simple copy that requires more refined, smaller movements.

Acquisition of Skill in Spelling. The acquisition of a spelling vocabulary is an individual matter. The child needs to be able to perceive the relationship that exists between the sound of the word and its written form, the inter-association of its parts, and its meaning. When long words can be spelled phoenetically, children have little difficulty in learning to spell them. Yet some basic words of one or two syllables are difficult to spell. Such words should be learned as early as possible and through their use become fixed. Other words probably are mastered best when they are learned in context, rather than on isolated word lists.

Need for Grammar Usage. A child's written language usually follows the form of expression used in oral language. The child who, during the preschool years, has been exposed to correct grammatical usage usually carries his habit patterns over into written composition. Since more flexibility of construction is permitted in spoken language than in written, the child needs to be guided toward expressing his ideas in clear, terse form, giving attention to sentence and paragraph sequences, appropriate terminology, and other elements of comprehensible written material.

During the child's early learning in written expression, emphasis needs to be placed on the use of short, simple sentences that contain no more than one idea. There is difference of opinion concerning the value of a detailed study of grammar. At one time, there was attention given to the rote memorization and the application of many complicated grammatical rules. Recently, some educators believe ᵗhat a child is helped to improve his written expression if he knows why he should follow certain basic rules of agreement of subject and verb or of noun and pronoun, and of relationships between main and subordinate clauses. Consequently, grammar is treated from a practical or functional viewpoint, rather than as a formal study of rules that may be memorized but not understood.

Expressing Ideas in Written Form. A child's purpose in writing is associated almost entirely with daily experiences in his environment. Nevertheless, no matter how simple a child's attempt at written expression may be, he must have something to say that is worthwhile and say it in correct grammatical form. This requires a great deal of practice for the average child.

The child may have interesting ideas but lack mastery of the mechanics of writing, or he may have developed relatively correct form but have little or nothing to say. In either instance, one activity interferes with the other, and he needs careful teacher guidance lest he become a sterile or rambling writer. This instructional guidance should include directing of the child's attention to both the content and the style or mechanics of the written material.

Individuals differ widely in ability to acquire skill in written composition. This is true of adults as well as of children. Mental abilities, motor control, and memory and imagination as well as a fine sense of word usage and balanced sentence structure are among the factors that affect the degree of skill a child may be expected eventually to attain.

Whether superior ability in written expression, especially in the field of creative writing, has a hereditary base is not certain. It is true that effective production seems to "run" in families. Early and continued favorable environment, and encouragement, as well as inherited potentialities may be responsible for the differences that exist.

CHAPTER 5

Mental Development and Intelligence

Mental development and physical maturation are components of an integrated whole rather than two coexisting entities. Since the existence of the mental aspect of development can be recognized only through its functioning in the observable behavior of an individual, it is more difficult to understand, control, or determine than is the progress of physical maturation, which can be measured from the prenatal period onward.

Various factors affect mental development. The constitution of the inherited nervous system determines the rate and extent of possible development. Certain other physical conditions or individual and environmental factors may accelerate or retard mental progress. Disturbances of the total personality pattern also may interfere with more or less "normal" development.

BEGINNINGS OF AWARENESS

Mental growth is characterized by a synthesized organization of various developmental patterns which show themselves early in the child's behavior and are different from what may be considered simple reflex responses. The mental activity of the very young child represents an area of development which helps him to integrate his behavior patterns as, even then, he is striving towards psychological maturity. At first this so-called mental activity is no more than the beginning of awareness of himself and of elements in his environment.

Behavior patterning is evidenced before birth. Fetuses differ from one another in the kind and amount of their activity. Both bodily and behavioral organization is taking place during the prenatal period. The heart begins to beat; some sensory activity develops; the beginnings of respiration are present; and body movements are experienced. All these activities contribute to the repertory of behavior patterns but cannot be said to reflect mental activity as that term is used to describe the behavior of the child during his later stages of development.

The expression of individuality shown during the neonatal period is the result of the beginning of mental growth that was taking place during the prenatal period. Inherent maturational mechanisms determine the extent and direction of this behavior development. The structure of the nervous system begins to grow during the prenatal period. As it continues to grow and develop before and after birth, the "mind" grows with it. The nervous system permits the patterning process. Mental growth produces patterned behavior and brings about changes in the patterns.

The newborn infant is helpless and dependent, but he is able to attend to certain forms of stimulation and seems able to learn early and quickly. The attitudes he forms, the kind of socialization he develops, and the various ways in which he satisfies his needs and desires grow out of his beginning potentialities of awareness. How his mental processes will develop from this point onward will depend upon his own pattern of growth and the stimuli provided by his environment.

MENTAL DEVELOPMENT DURING CHILDHOOD

Mental development includes the continued formation and functioning of patterned responses. As the child develops from birth onward, changes take place in his mental reactions that give indications of progress from ability to respond to simple stimuli toward the functioning of complex mental operations.

The extent of intellectual growth of an individual is limited to the number and kind of complex mental processes in which he can engage successfully. Mental activity, as such, comprises various aspects of mental reaction and association. These generally are categorized as sensation, perception, memory, imagination, and reasoning. These various aspects do not develop in isolation or function independently. Rather are they interdependent and give evidence of much interaction. As the child's behavioral pattern progresses, mental development shows itself in the overt expression of such interactions.

Mental development is continuous. Hence, the various stages of progress give little if any evidence of marked changes. Development, however, is more rapid during one age period than during another. There may be greater development in one area of mental activity than in others at different ages.

The Young Child. As has been said earlier, the baby gives little, if any, evidence of what may be referred to as intelligent behavior. He possesses, however, all the sensory equipment that can provide potential raw material out of which the complex aspects of his personality will develop.

During the period from infancy to about three years of age, the child's needs increase and become more definite and more specialized. He also is becoming more selective in the ways that these needs shall be satisfied. His behavior indicates that he wants attention, and he does what he can to secure approval. He wants to be recognized as an individual.

Interest in Things. The child early begins to show curiosity about his immediate surroundings and the people with whom he comes into contact. The tendency to make-believe may also have its beginnings at this age period. The child has a tendency to personify the objects that are in the world about him. To him they become living entities with which he may identify himself. If the child is told a story about a bear or sees a bear in the zoo, he is impelled to engage in activities that to him resemble bear behavior. He may respond in the same way to experiences with a train, a bird, or his father or mother.

Realization of Self. The child also is becoming an individualist and is becoming aware of the difference between *I* and *you*. He engages in much attention-getting behavior. Typical of this behavior is the negativistic attitude expressed in an emphatic "No!" to many or most questions asked him or requests made of him. He sometimes responds in action that is affirmative as he vocalizes aloud the negative response.

The Preschool Child. During the years between three and six the child's mental abilities develop rapidly. This is shown through his use of articulate speech. He not only learns to use words as such but also understands their meaning.

The child seeks and utilizes many sensory and perceptual experiences. As his perceptual powers increase he seeks more and more sensory stimulation. His curiosity is awakened and he shows keen

47

interest in that which is new, and different from his accustomed surroundings. He continues the life of make-believe. In association with other children he will reproduce in great detail many family or other social settings. To play house or to play school is an important means of developing mental qualities.

By the time a child is ready to enter the elementary school at the age of six or thereabout, his mental abilities have matured sufficiently to provide a foundation for the building of patterns of thinking and behavior that will result in individualization in his personality development. He not only can function as an individual but also has achieved the capacity to share experiences with others. In his own simple way he thinks for himself but at the same time appears to respect the judgment of others.

Later Childhood Development. The child in the elementary school responds to stimuli that are intellectual as well as social. His mental abilities continue to develop under the stimulus of his new and enlarging environment.

During these years the child's sensory equipment becomes well developed. His perceptual powers increase in keenness and accuracy. Gradually, he can be expected to concentrate for a longer time on psychologically simple material. His earlier somewhat photographic memory is giving way to increased ability to function more logically, and his imaginative abilities now are directed toward creative thinking.

During the preschool period, a child's intellectual pursuits, including his interests, plans, and thoughts, tend to concern those persons near him in time and age. Now, however, interest expands to include people and things in the world at large. The child comes to admire persons who have become public figures and sometimes regards them as ideals to be imitated. This is one of the aspects of intellectual growth.

The team work engaged in by the older child shows an increased capacity for social interchange on a maturing mental level. As a child acquires increased capacity for sharing ideas with others, he also continues to be concerned with his own desires and interests. His personal thoughts, feelings, desires, and problems will continue to be peculiarly his own throughout his developing years. He retains his individuality as the process of socialization goes steadily on. In effect, his individuality is extended through his intellectual life as that relates to the welfare of others.

48

Capacity for Generalizing. The young child is able to imagine, to daydream, and to engage in fantasy. Later he is capable of applying both inductive and deductive reasoning to his experiences. A child of elementary school age can think and reason. The kind of reasoning done by him is likely to vary with the particular problem by which he is challenged. He may be quite logical in the utilization of the thought process in the solution of one problem but not in dealing with another if it is unlike the first. Given the data necessary to the solution of a problem, he probably will be able to generalize and to offer adequate solutions or conclusions.

Children's knowledge and understanding are influenced by what parents and especially what other children say. Many of the superstitions that are prevalent today are passed on to children who accept them as fact. Some children, however, learn early to evaluate, whereas others accept whatever is told them. If a child seems to believe adult misrepresentation of the truth, the same adult who originally gave him the false information may wonder why the child is so gullible.

THE NATURE OF INTELLIGENCE

The study of intelligence is an area of research that continues to challenge anyone who attempts to explain completely or adequately the functioning of intelligence. Although a great deal of data relative to the development of intelligence has been collected, psychologists find it difficult to define intelligence in specific terms. A part of the difficulty lies in the fact that intelligence is a concept and therefore lends itself to great variation of interpretation. Satisfactory headway has been made, however, in the measurement of intelligence to the extent that behavior can be described as *more* or *less* intelligent in given situations.

Meaning of Intelligence. According to Thorndike, basic to an individual's degree of intelligence or of intelligent behavior is his degree of ability in such mental operations as attention span, recognition, retention and recall, inductive and deductive reasoning, abstraction and generalization, and organization as these respond to the learning process. Hence, Thorndike defines intelligence as the "power of good responses from the point of view of truth or fact." In their definitions of intelligence, other psychologists emphasize variously the ability to adjust to novel

49

situations, the degree of ability to think in terms of abstract ideas, and the capacity to learn or to profit by experience.

Stoddard formulated a descriptive statement of intelligence as "the ability to undertake activities that are characterized by (1) difficulty, (2) complexity, (3) abstractness, (4) economy (speed), (5) adaptiveness to a goal, (6) social value, and (7) the emergence of originals (inventiveness), and to maintain such activities under conditions that demand a concentration of energy and a resistance to emotional forces."

Factors Affecting Intelligence. Individual differences in degree of mental acuity or intelligence can be explained to some extent in terms of certain inherent characteristics as these are influenced by environmental conditions. Except in special cases, however, it is difficult to isolate any one factor as the sole cause of intellectual status. Among the more generally accepted bases of differences can be included: health and physical development, sex, and social and economic conditions.

Health and Physical Development. Physical and mental health status may be related to a child's ability to gain desirable achievement in mental activity. The delicate child may not possess enough energy to engage in mental activity to the extent that he achieves success. Physical defects, such as retarded or incomplete maturation of brain cells, may result in subnormal intelligence. Blindness or near-blindness and deafness are other physical handicaps that may interfere with observable intelligent behavior. Conditions such as glandular imbalance, enlarged adenoids, and diseased tonsils also affect mental acuity.

An emotional block may interfere with a child's ability to give evidence of the intelligence which he actually possesses. Fear or lack of self-confidence, induced by one or more previous unsatisfactory situations, may cause the child to retreat from a new situation that offers mental challenge.

Although unfavorable health conditions may seem to affect mental status, actual mental ability is not related in any appreciable degree to remediable health handicaps. In those cases in which the physical or mental health handicap can be removed or mitigated a decided improvement in intellectual behavior can be observed.

Sex. It is a popular belief that boys and men are more intelligent than girls and women. High school boys are supposed to excel in more abstract areas of learning such as mathematics and the physical sciences. Men are presumed to be more mechanical-minded than women.

These differences between the sexes, to the extent to which they give evidence of existing, can be traced to early environmental conditions, especially in homes where the experiences of boys and girls reflect the acceptance of such sex differences. The administration of tests of intelligence to the same age groups of boys and girls appears to yield the following general results:

1. During early childhood there is little if any difference in mental ability between the sexes.

2. Because of their advantage in rate of physical growth, girls seem to surpass boys during the later childhood and early adolescent years.

3. During later adolescence, boys may show a slight superiority over girls but the difference is negligible, especially since there are wide divergences among the members of either sex.

4. Analyses of performance on specific items of intelligence tests appear to show that there is slight superiority of boys in questions that involve mathematical material and scientific concepts, and that girls excel in materials that deal more directly with the humanities. Such differences, as suggested earlier, may be caused by differences in experience.

Social and Economic Conditions. Since the home plays a significant role in the early developmental years of a child, it can be expected that home conditions will exercise considerable influence upon the child's background of experience and his consequent behavior and attitudes. The activities, interests, and financial status of parents and of other adults in the neighborhood environment may provide for the child poor, relatively meager, or extremely rich series of experiences. The amount and kind of mental challenge to which the young person is exposed, at various periods of his life, determine to a great degree the amount and kind of mental activity in which he engages.

Apparently low socioeconomic status may result from factors outside the immediate control of parents, as, for example, during a period of general economic depression. The parents themselves may possess a high degree of intelligence but be the victims of circumstances. In such cases, the child's inherited intellectual potential usually is able to assist him to surmount unfavorable living conditions, and he gives evidence of intelligent behavior in spite of meager social and economic background.

MEASUREMENT OF INTELLIGENCE

The best method for evaluating a person's degree of intelligence is probably that of observing his behavior in day-by-day situations that challenge his ability to perform successfully. It is not always possible, however, to observe an individual in a sufficiently large number of such situations, if it is necessary to make a relatively quick decision concerning his mental ability. Hence, a technique must be provided for measuring intelligence quickly and with relative accuracy. The construction of such instruments of evaluation is one of the most important contributions of psychological study. Many tests in this area of evaluation have been devised that vary in form and in degree of reliability and validity. Some are more suitable than others for a given age level.

The Development of Intelligence Tests. During the nineteenth century, various attempts were made to evaluate degree of sensory acuity, rote memory, and the like. It was not until the present century, however, that attention was directed by psychologists to the construction of instruments designed to attempt the measurement of intelligence.

The Individual Intelligence Test. The first published intelligence test was constructed in France by Alfred Binet, a psychologist, and Theodore Simon. This test was devised for the purpose of discovering the mental status of French children who were failing to earn success in school achievement. The test was evolved originally in 1905 and revisedin 1908, and again in 1911. The Binet-Simon Test of Mental Ability is an individual test of performance, the scores of which are interpreted in terms of mental age. The constructors of the test emphasized the need of good rapport established between the subject tested and the administrator of the test. Since directions are given orally and responses are oral, written, or manipulatory, the reliability of test results depends upon the care with which the test is administered.

The Binet-Simon Test has been adapted for use by various other countries. In America, adaptations of the test were made by Goddard (1911), Kuhlmann (1912), and Terman (1916). The Terman adaptation was revised in 1937, and is now known as the Terman-Merrill revision of the Stanford-Binet Scale. The test has several forms. The following are examples of the items included in Form L of the revised test that are supposed to measure intelligent behavior of the average or normal five-year-old.

Picture Completion: Man
Paper Folding: Triangle
Definitions
Memory for Sentences
Counting Four Objects

The Group Intelligence Test. Individual intelligence testing is time-consuming. The drafting of large groups of men for army service during World War I gave rise to the problem of allocating soldiers to specific jobs for which they might be suited. A relatively efficient and quick method of discovering individual abilities was needed. To meet this need, a selected committee of psychologists constructed two forms of intelligence tests that could be administered to large groups of soldiers at one time. These tests are known as the Army Alpha for men who could read and write English, and the Army Beta for illiterates or those men who could not read or write English. The format and the items included in these tests have served as models for the subsequent construction of tests to be used for all school levels and for adults.

Classification of Intelligence Tests. At present there are many available forms of intelligence tests, more or less valid and reliable. These tests have been constructed to meet various purposes, age levels, and methods of administration. Group paper-and-pencil tests are among those most widely used and represent tests that are appropriate for use in the elementary and secondary schools, and with adults. These, for the most part, are *verbal* tests in which the testee reads and responds to questions dealing with vocabulary, mathematical concepts, relationships, and information.

Performance tests may take the form either of individual administration or of group administration. In either case, the child is asked to manipulate testing materials. Performance tests are especially valuable for testing very young children or non-English-speaking individuals. The Revised Army Beta is especially good for use with foreign children or adults. A few of the more widely used tests will be described briefly.

Individual Intelligence Tests. The Terman-Merrill revision of the Binet-Simon Scale is one of the most reliable instruments available for measuring the mental ability of individuals between the ages of two years through adulthood. It is especially suitable for measuring the intelligence of elementary school children.

Attempts have been made to construct tests that will yield reliable measures of the mental ability of very young children. Two of these tests are: Cattell's Test for the Measurement of Intelligence of Infants and Young Children for ages of two through thirty months, and the Minnesota Preschool Test for ages of eighteen months through six years. Good as tests on this age level may be, the results of their administration should not be considered predictive of the later intelligence status of the child tested.

Another individual intelligence test for children that is gaining in popularity is the Wechsler Intelligence Scale for Children. Also much used, especially in psychological clinics, is the Wechsler-Bellevue Test which was constructed for use with adolescents and adults. The Wechsler tests include various types of verbal and performance materials.

Group Intelligence Tests. Group tests permit larger numbers of individuals to be tested, and are meeting with general approval. These tests are more easily adapted to use with the older child, adolescent, or adult. There are several good group tests, however, for use with children of elementary school age or younger.

The Goodenough Draw-A-Man Scale is a type of performance test devised for use with children between the ages of three and thirteen. It is best adapted to the preschool years.

Primary Mental Abilities Tests have been constructed by the Thurstones to measure some of the fundamental mental abilities. Different factors can be measured for different ages from three through seventeen years. Results can be expressed in profile form.

The California Test of Mental Maturity yields the usual index measure or I.Q. In this test the I.Q. can be obtained through the administration of materials that include either language or non-language items. These have been constructed to measure the abilities of individuals ranging in age level from the kindergarten period to adulthood. The results of these tests also can be expressed in a diagnostic profile.

The Kuhlmann-Anderson Intelligence Test is used widely with school groups from the kindergarten through the twelfth grade. It is arranged in nine consecutive booklets, which maximizes comparability of the development of intelligence from age to age. A revised form of this test has appeared recently.

Predictive Value of Intelligence Tests. There is a relatively high degree of consistency in intelligence-test results from year to year, from the age of five onward. The value of test results increases as the child goes on through school, especially during the upper elementary and junior high school years. Test results are commonly used as a basis for homogeneous grouping and as a means to discover specific learning difficulties and needs among children.

THE EXTREMES IN INTELLIGENCE

Among any unselected group of children there usually can be found those who deviate considerably from what can be referred to as the "normally intelligent child." A child who gives evidence of behavior that is definitely inferior to what can be expected for his age period of mental development is termed *feeble-minded.* Similarly, a child whose reactions indicate that his mental status is far superior to that of his age group is known as *gifted.* A child in either of these categories is sometimes referred to as a *mental deviate.*

Feeble-minded Children. A feeble-minded child can be found on any socioeconomic level, but especially at the lower levels. His incomplete mental maturation usually is apparent from birth or begins to show itself at an early age. Social subnormality is characteristic of his behavior. In general, feeble-mindedness is characterized by constitutional deficiency, intellectual retardation, developmental arrest, and social inferiority.

Feeble-minded children and adults are classified according to three groupings: idiots, imbeciles, and morons.

Idiots. The lowest group represents the most severe degree of mental deficiency. Even as adults, idiots cannot care for their personal needs, protect themselves from harm, or participate in the simplest of occupational tasks. These characeristics of idiots begin to show themselves during early childhood. During their life span, which usually does not extend beyond the thirties, their mental age is that of a child up to three years of age, and mental development is arrested at about six or eight years of age.

Imbeciles. The degree of deficiency is less pronounced among imbeciles. An imbecile can be taught to care for his personal needs, protect himself in some situations, and master routine assignments under close supervision. Under present conditions he appears to be unable to benefit appreciably from academic instruction or to acquire any but simple occupational skills. Mental maturity is attained at about ten to twelve years of age, but the mental-age range is somewhere between three and seven years.

Morons. The moron group represents the highest grade of feeble-mindedness, and should not be confused with the intelligence group represented in the behavior of the slow but normally intelligent child. Under favorable conditions a moron is capable of caring for his own needs, may master the rudiments of school learning, and may acquire a limited degree of skill in some of the simpler occupations. His social success is precarious since he lacks social judgment. Mental maturity is reached between eight and twelve years. Social maturity is complete, although inadequate, at about twenty years of age.

Gifted Children. Children with ability to think, reason, and utilize the higher mental processes in making judgments, and children who are especially endowed with talent for creative or inventive activities, are considered to be gifted children.

Gifted children come from all racial stocks. Both sexes are included in this group, with boys showing a slight superiority over girls. They represent all kinds of backgrounds and homes, although the majority appear to have experienced favorable socioeconomic status. The gifted child's classroom attitudes usually are satisfactory, and he gives evidence of superior performance in academic school work. He also is usually superior physically as well as psychologically and tends to throw his extra energy into his activities. Studies in the field seem to reveal that traits of the gifted are inherited and that training can develop but not create them.

Some psychologists include in the group of gifted children those who earn an intelligence quotient of 130 or above on a reliable and valid intelligence test. Others would place this specific rating at 140 or higher. In a school population of a thousand children there may be expected to be ten children with I.Q.'s of 130 or higher and five with I.Q.'s of 140 or better.

Problems of Adjustment. A father and mother who have discovered that their child has ability far beyond that of the children of his age often emphasize this fact to the detriment of the child. For example, when friends visit the home, the child is invited to exhibit his special talent. This usually affects his attitude adversely. After a time he no longer may desire to be the family entertainer. He may develop an attitude of resentment that becomes intensified when his parents insist on his performing for their guests. Evidence of superiority in a child should be recognized but not overemphasized. Regardless of the ability, creativeness cannot be expected to flow constantly in even currents.

The gifted child early shows signs of leadership. He understands relationships and expects other children to play games according to his rules. He sometimes displays aggressiveness that often is attributed to lack of training. In many instances this attitude can be traceable to parental encouragement of self-expression. Consequently, he may have adjustment handicaps to overcome when he enters school. To help him, his parents need to give as much attention to the development of social attitudes as they do to his traits of cleverness.

CHAPTER 6

Development of Emotional Behavior

An individual's behavior in any given situation is likely to be motivated by a greater or lesser degree of tenderness, joy, sorrow, fear, anger, resentment, jealousy, awe, or any other one of various inner responses to the impact of the situation upon the personality of the individual. It is possible for him not to recognize fully the underlying reasons for his behavior. It may be difficult for him to express in words his inner reactions.

BASES OF EMOTIONAL BEHAVIOR

Inner behavior-motivating reactions do not exist in isolation, but display themselves as entities that can be classified objectively. They represent a kind of fusion of the effects upon a person of the many stimuli to which he is exposed and which have come to be either satisfying or annoying to himself. These inner reactions are referred to as the *emotions*. They exercise a powerful influence upon the life pattern of an individual.

Meaning of Emotion. An emotion can be defined briefly as a stirred-up state of the organism. The emotional state embodies feeling tones which are accompanied by marked physiological changes that include both the visceral and the peripheral areas. There is tension, there is release, and there are overt responses. Glandular changes may show themselves in appropriate behavior.

As an overt expression of the particular emotional state that has been aroused, a person may pale or flush, he may laugh or weep, he may retreat or move forward, he may embrace or attack. The perception of a situation as an emotion-arousing stimulus is essential to feelings basic to emotional response. The physiological reactions then are accompanied by inner drives toward action of one kind or another. The form that the action may take is influenced by experience.

An emotion is expressed when an individual is stirred up mentally and physiologically to the extent that there is a generalized inner adjustment, accompanied by strong feeling tones. This dynamic experience is a psychological reaction that, if reasonably controlled, operates for the welfare of the individual.

Stimulation of Emotions. Individuals differ in the extent to which a particular stimulus may be recognized as emotion-arousing. The arousal of an emotion, as well as its intensity when it has been aroused, depends upon various factors that are operative at the time. These include the individual's health status, his attitudes, interests, desires, and ideals, and the degree of his self-control and self-understanding.

If, for example, a person is generally interested in human welfare, he may become genuinely concerned about the death toll of a disease or a war but do nothing about it. When, however, a member of his own family is a victim of the disease or is a war casualty, this person may become so emotionally aroused that he is impelled to take action that may alleviate the situation for others.

Not only the stimulus but also the attitude of the person stimulated determines whether this or that emotion will be aroused. The same stimulus at one time may be a strong emotion-arouser for a person, and at another time affect him very little. For example, a person who is alone in a house at night, especially if this is an uncommon experience, may become so overcome by fear caused by sounds resulting from the cooling off of the house that he may be impelled to run to a neighbor's home for protection from someone who, he thinks, must be trying to get into the house. If, however, the family is at home, the individual, hearing the same kind of noises, may recognize them for what they are and be in no way disturbed by them.

The same stimulus also may arouse different emotions under different circumstances. A person may be delighted to have a respected and admired colleague address him by his first name, but may resent it if a person whom he considers to be inferior to himself dares to do so.

An emotion is likely to continue so long as the stimulus that aroused it commands the attention of the responder. The stimulus must be removed to eliminate or to change an emotion. This characteristic of emotional response makes possible the quick change that is experienced by an individual as he hates at one moment and displays affectionate behavior at the next.

Physiological Changes and Emotions. Stimuli that arouse emotional experience produce certain visceral changes that are measurable, and skeletal changes that are observable. The physiologist can study the sudden stopping of digestive movements, the forcing of extra blood into the extremities, increased blood pressure, decreased flow of saliva, and changes in endocrinal secretion. The lay person may observe the quickened pace, the rapid breathing, flushes, flow of tears, choking of voice, or bulging of eyes. These physiological changes do not produce the emotion but accompany the emotional experience and aid the individual in his adjustment to it.

The internal secretions of the endocrine glands affect the autonomic nervous system and produce rapid physiological changes. In turn, the emotional process is quickened. The secretion of the adrenal glands, for example, relaxes the smooth muscles, sends blood to the surface of the body, releases glycogen into the blood stream, increases the heartbeat, and contracts the blood vessels. Normal functioning of the ductless glands is required for desirable emotional stability. Overactivity or underactivity of the thyroid gland may overexcite the individual or cause him to become sluggish, respectively.

THE DEVELOPING EMOTIONS

The potentialities of so-called emotionalized behavior are present at birth. At first, they appear to consist of diffused feeling tones. Later, they gradually take on definite reaction patterns that can be recognized as representing one or another emotional state.

Emotional Diffusion during Infancy. The infant probably experiences no more than relative degrees of well-being or disturbance that are stimulated in great part by the extent to which his physiological needs are satisfied. When he is well fed and comfortable, he coos, gurgles, or falls asleep, thus evincing a pleasant state of well-being. Contrariwise, when he is hungry or experiencing physical discomfort, he cries, squirms, and displays generally restless behavior. He soon learns how to gain adult attention.

The satisfied baby engages in outgoing behavior. He may extend his arms in a gesture that seems to indicate that he wants to be picked up and cuddled. A strange or unpleasant situation causes him to withdraw and to give other indications of annoyance. Hence, although feeling tones probably arise during early infancy, the actual emotional experience of the young child cannot be definitely classified by observers of his behavior.

Beginnings of Emotionalized Behavior. During babyhood, emotional patterns gradually emerge. According to the results of psychological study, the developmental pattern begins with excitement and distress, followed by fear, anger, and disgust. By the end of the first year, behavior is displayed that would seem to indicate the emotional states of affection and elation, and later of jealousy.

Emotionalized Behavior of the Older Child. As the child acquires greater understanding of his relationships with people and things, the effect upon him of his day-by-day satisfactions and annoyances, stemming from attention-getting and thwarting, takes on patterns of expressed attitudes that can be recognized as emotions.

Changes in Emotional Expression. The young child is likely to display a general gross expression of emotionalism. He squeals with delight; lashes out at everything around him when he is angered; cries and runs to an adult for protection when he experiences a fear-stimulating situattion. As he matures, he learns to focus his emotional behavior upon the person or object responsible for his disturbed state. He also acquires, through training and imitation of adults, the ability to gain greater control of his behavior and express his emotions in more subtle and refined ways.

Role of Imitation. Imitation plays an important role in the development of a child's emotionalized behavior. The attitude displayed by adults toward potential emotion-arousers influences greatly a child's probable reaction in similar situations. The child of emotionally well-balanced parents usually learns early to control his own emotions.

A parent who indulges in temper tantrums should not be surprised when his child meets tantrum with tantrum. The fears of surrounding adults are reflected in the child's behavior. Many of the likes and dislikes that seem to be habitual for a child have their roots in the expressed emotionalized attitudes of his parents or of his other older associates.

General Emotional Patterns. Children's emotionally aroused behavior tends to give evidence of certain more or less general patterns that grow out of experiences common to most children. As in other aspects of development, however, some individual differences can be observed.

Differences between the Child and the Adult. The average child and the average adult probably give expression to similar emotional states. There are differences between them, however, in the extent to which a given situation is reacted to emotionally and in the characteristics of the emotional reaction.

Because of his relatively meager body of experiences, a child may become either more or less aroused by a set of circumstances. A potentially dangerous situation may be recognized and reacted to by the adult but mean nothing to a child. Yet a relatively insignificant denial of his wishes may greatly disturb a child, whereas the adult has learned that one cannot always have one's desires satisfied.

There are other differences between the child's and the adult's emotionalized reactions. Both may experience intense emotionalism. Generally, the child's emotional state at the moment spends itself in complete emotional expression. The adult has learned through experience that his immediate emotional reaction needs to be controlled. Hence, the child "gets over" a particular emotional state much more quickly than does the adult.

The child can be distracted from the emotion-arousing experience, especially one that stimulates fear or anger, to a pleasant activity. He then relaxes and shifts, sometimes with surprising speed, to the expression of delight, affection, and general well-being. The adult, on the contrary, may control the over expression of his emotional state but continue to experience the emotion for a long period of time, giving expression to it from time to time in more or less subtle but intense fashion.

Emotional Differences among Children. Not only does children's emotionalized behavior differ from that of adults, but it also differs among children of the same age or maturational status. Unless one knows a particular child very well, the latter's emotional responses cannot be predicted with certainty. Each child develops characteristic forms of reaction to emotion-arousing stimuli. The response to a fear-inducing or strange situation, for example, may be attempted withdrawal, cautious behavior, or extreme aggression.

62

Differences in emotional response reflect differences that are inherent in the individual or that stem from environmental conditions or influences. The daily stimuli provided by parents and other adults close to the child have much to do with the patterning of his emotional behavior.

Adult Responsibility for Children's Emotions. A child responds to adult attitudes toward his emotionalized behavior. He learns that emotional outbursts are frowned upon by those about him, since he meets social disapproval and sometimes punishment for an unbridled expression of an emotion. It is characteristic even of a young child to display intense emotion more frequently in the home than he does outside the home.

Parental Attitudes. A child experiences conflict in many parent-child situations. Parents thrill to the emotional excitement of the child when they stimulate it. They also set up many restraints when they want to curtail childish enthusiasm. Consequently, an emotional outburst may receive parental approval at one time, but may be met with criticism, disapproval, or varying forms of punish-ment at another time.

The child comes to understand that certain forms of emotionalized behavior are acceptable but that others are not. When he cries, screams, throws things, or strikes another, he usually receives the kind of disapproval that helps him to learn quickly that such behavior is not acceptable in any group or situation. In a relatively strict home he also learns that he must constrain himself when he is pleased. The joyful expression of shouting with glee or of clapping his hands is denied him. Regardless of the amount of restraint that is exercised in relation to a child's emotional behavior, it is important that he learn early not to meet feelings of thwarting or frustration by engaging in a temper tantrum. This kind of behavior will not be tolerated by his elders or by his playmates.

Parental attitudes account for more emotional disturbances among children than is commonly realized. To give more attention to one child than to another is difficult to avoid but is damaging to both. To neglect children or to be away from home a great deal; to be overanxious about children; to talk about their ailments in the presence of other children; to overprotect children; to overpermit children to do as they desire; to deny children proper experiences of growing up; and to make them the idol of the home — all contribute to the development of undesirable emotional behavior. Emotional maturity comes through wholesome attitudes of parents toward permitting children to act and to think for themselves under supervision that is neither too rigid nor too permissive.

Influences outside the Home. A child's emotional habits are affected by his associations with people outside the home, as well as by the members of his family. He imitates the behavior of other children or of adults. For example, to allow a child to be with a highly emotional playmate for several hours tends to increase his own emotionality. Conversely, association with a calm, well-controlled person helps the child to achieve control of his own emotions.

Investigators have found that social status and emotional stability are closely related. Greater maladjustment and more emotional instability are likely to be found among children who have a poor social background than is the case for children who are reared in homes that represent a better social status. More satisfactory adjustments to day-by-day situations usually are made by the latter group.

If a child of school age fails in a subject, is overage for his group, or cannot seem to conform to certain school regulations, he tends to become emotionally unstable. The drive toward successful achievement and social recognition is strong in the child. To the extent that he can fulfill these drives he will be a healthy, happy, and emotionally well-adjusted child.

If a young person feels that he does not receive the social approval that he believes he deserves or if his interests and desires are thwarted, he may be moved to engage in varying degrees of aggressive behavior or withdrawal. He may turn to a substitute response, such as daydreaming or rationalization, which rarely yield satisfying results. Some young people, however, can be sufficiently motivated so that they will achieve control of their emotions and overcome adverse conditions.

Other Factors of Influence. Differences in a child's emotional reactions can be explained in terms of conditions that lie outside the direct influence of parents and other close associates of the child but that should be recognized by adults as possible causes of the arousal of emotionalism in the child.

A child's health status is closely related to his emotional reactions. Good health predisposes toward healthful and desirable emotional expression. One or another form of emotional disturbance is likely to be displayed by a child who suffers from malnutrition, digestive disturbances, diseased tonsils, defective eyes, poor teeth, or other ailments.

Extreme fatigue predisposes toward emotional disturbances. The active child uses up a great deal of energy during the course of the day. Hence, he needs food and rest at regular intervals. If these are delayed, he usually becomes very much annoyed. When a child becomes tired or is overtaxed or overexcited, he is predisposed to indulge in undesirable emotional behavior such as temper tantrums. The play and rest periods need to be well spaced for the very young child. Fatigue predisposes to irritability and other forms of undesirable emotional behavior at every stage of childhood, but is most serious during the early years.

SOME SPECIFIC EMOTIONS

It is generally accepted that the emotions add richness to life. The various emotional states have value for an individual if they are controlled in such ways that they can serve the individual rather than destroy him. The extent to which an adult gives evidence of mastery over his emotions is rooted in his emotional experiences, their stimulation and their treatment, from early childhood through adolescence.

The child is affectionate and outgoing. He also displays a real and imaginary fear. He is moved to anger. How various emotional states are aroused, the behavior that results from their arousal, and some of the ways in which they can be controlled will be discussed briefly.

Affection or the Tender Emotions. Affection, love, or the tender emotions represent outgoing reactions that are directed toward a person, object, or situation which is associated with pleasant or satisfying experiences.

An infant welcomes the experience of being held and fondled. His characteristic behavior responses to this kind of experience are smiling, laughing, or playful behavior. These early signs of affection do not represent an innate emotional response of the child directed toward relatives. He learns to have affection for his parents or those who care for him or play with him. The child's affective attitude toward another person depends upon the treatment of himself given to him by the other.

The receiving of affectionate attention from others in his day-by-day living may be one of the most important factors of the young child's emotions. He needs the feeling of security that accompanies affectionate behavior toward him on the part of an adult. During his growing-up period, the child needs to experience the satisfaction of knowing that he is liked and wanted.

As the child's social world enlarges, he gradually transfers some of the affection that heretofore had been centered in the family unit to other children and adults outside the home. Parents who attempt to monopolize the child's affection may interfere seriously with his later wholesome relationships. Emotional weaning is necessary for good social development.

Loyalties among members of a family, a school, a club or other social organization, or a political party are based upon affective attitudes that often may arise from time to time. A child may quarrel with one or another member of his family but, when put to the test, demonstrate great affection for the other. Overt expressions need not be continuous. Occasional hostility is normal among healthy, alert children. Aggression by an outsider, however, will unite them in their opposition to him.

Affection is a two-way process. Not only should the child receive affection, but he should be trained to become interested in the welfare of others. Acts of kindliness should be performed for his interest and welfare. At the same time, he should be helped to develop the habit of doing things for others that are concerned with their well-being rather than with his own self-centered interests.

The degree of cordiality that exists between a child and his parents may have a significant effect upon his later attitudes. Too often, deep-seated prejudices and fears grow out of a child's concealed attitude of hostility toward parents during his formative years. A child who is reared in a home in which he experiences parental respect and affection accompanied by appropriate companionship and a sharing of responsibility usually displays co-operative and friendly attitudes toward his associates outside the home. Unless, during his later life, he is subjected to unpleasant experiences with people who are generally suspicious and unco-operative, he is likely to remain an outgoing, kindly person.

Love as Associated with Sex. Strong affection and physical attraction combine to represent the emotion usually referred to as love between the sexes. The normal, healthy adolescent experiences great emotional satisfaction from companionship with a member of the other sex whom he admires and about whom he is sexually excited. The adolescent or young adult may become attracted to

66

one or more members of the opposite sex as he is progressing toward full adult status. His behavior during this exploratory period is conditioned by the emotional control he has acquired during childhood and the ideals of conduct that have become habitual for him.

During childhood days, the young person usually is not too much concerned with love between the sexes. He may respond, however, to sexual stimulation. There are many behavior problems that center around love and sex which require careful guidance. Among the most significant of these problems during the childhood years are those associated with masturbation and sex play, and, later, homosexual activities.

It is normal for a baby to explore all the parts of his body that he can reach. Thumb- and toe-sucking and playing with his genitals give the baby a kind of physical satisfaction that may cause him to continue the practices unless substitute stimuli, such as a soft toy, can be substituted. Parental concern over these activities should not take the form of a scolding or shock but rather of acceptance of a situation that needs patient handling, which includes distraction of the child from his own body to appropriate manipulatory toys.

Masturbation may occur at all age levels, especially among lonely children. It probably is more prevalent among boys than among girls, and usually occurs most frequently during the preschool years and adolescence. Masturbation during early childhood probably is not so harmful as it is during the adolescent period, especially in terms of undesirable psychological effects. Persistent and continuous masturbation during the teen years may lead to feelings of guilt or personal inadequacy that can interfere with normal sex attitudes and good martial adjustment.

Sex play engaged in by young children with members of either sex also is a kind of explorative activity that may have little significance. It may indicate that the children concerned are not provided with sufficient opportunity to engage in healthful play activities with peer groups.

Adolescents and young adults may form a strong attachment to a member of the same sex. Such attachments to older people, especially teachers, usually referred to as "crushes," are found among many high school girls and some high school boys. The young person admires the teacher very much and tends to imitate the latter's dress and mannerisms. If by so doing, the adolescent improves his own tastes in dress, as well as his manners, it is a good emotional experience. Unless the girl or boy annoys the beloved teacher by a doglike following around or by demands for attention, no harm is done.

Physical contact or sex play between two members of the same sex (homosexuality) is undesirable. This practice is more common among boys during later childhood years and adolescence than it is among girls, although it can be found among older adolescent and young adult girls. Since homosexuality is frowned upon by society in general, it has a harmful effect upon young people who practice it and also may interfere with desirable heterosexual development.

Anger and Aggressive Behavior. Resentment, anger, jealousy, or any other form of antisocial or aggressive reaction is commonly experienced, either mildly or more intensely, by most children as well as by adults. The emotion may be justified or it may arise out of personal feelings or insecurity. Whatever the cause may be, the resulting behavior can become socially undesirable, unless it is controlled.

Anger is a term used to describe emotional states ranging from the milder forms of resentment to rage. A child learns early that through angry outbursts he can gain attention from others or achieve a desired goal. As the child grows and develops, situations that may arouse anger tend to increase in number and kind. Hence, he experiences more anger reactions with increased age.

Causes and Modes of Expression. Anger arises in situations in which the child's activities or plans are thwarted, or in which his possessions or his prestige are interfered with. The nature and extent of emotional expression vary with the conditions, the general state of the individual, and the particular situation in which it occurs. Age and sex play an important role in determining the particular reaction of the child in an anger-arousing situation. Individual differences become more pronounced during the progress of development.

If a child's bodily activities are restrained, if his movements are interfered with, if his wishes are thwarted, or if insufficient attention is given him, his resulting behavior is likely to reflect a state of anger. When a child is thwarted, he may scream, pinch, bite, grab, stamp, cry, sulk, or throw things. Anger in childhood usually is expressed through generally aggressive behavior that is explosive in nature. Later, however, expressions of anger are aimed at a particular object or person. When the desires of an adult are thwarted or his activities interfered with, the emotional expression

68

may take the form of attack or verbalization, including profanity and criticism.

The angry child may express his emotionalized state by saying to his mother, "I hate you" or "I don't like you." The adolescent is more subtle in his expressions of anger, yet just as devastating. He makes use of sarcasm, ridicule, and innuendo.

In a violent outburst of temper the child may scream, kick, hold his breath, hit his head against the floor, throw things, or, if old enough, use strong invectives. A temper tantrum is a display of emotional behavior of this kind on the part of a child or older person for the purpose of getting what he wants. Temper tantrums may show themselves as early as fifteen months, but usually do not occur until the child is two or three years old. Then there is a period of decline until the age of two or three years old. Then there is a period of decline until the age of nine, at which time they tend to increase in frequency. During all these periods, boys are more likely to display temper tantrums than are girls.

The school-age child shows more control of anger than does the preschool child. Boys and sometimes girls, however, continue to exhibit antisocial emotional behavior as shown in their fighting, teasing, pushing, and other types of physical response during the elementary school years. Verbal expression, however, is coming into more frequent use at these ages and soon will replace, to a great extent, the more direct behavior-contact procedures. Any tantrum shown then is expressed in more refined behavior that, nevertheless, often is definite.

A child must learn to express his anger in such a way as to avoid social disapproval. In order for him to overcome anger, his attention should be directed to a stimulus unlike the one that has produced the existing emotional state. In this way he can be helped to substitute more pleasant feeling tones than those which he was experiencing. Consistent behavior by adults is important in dealing with control of anger. Both the child and the situation must be considered, since the same methods employed with different children by different adults may produce differing results.

The arousal of anger in a child is conditioned by his health and physical status and his behavior routines. The child's degree of immaturity also is a factor, but regular meals and sleeping periods, and opportunities to be active and to relax, tend to develop in the young child desirable attitudes of plesantness and feelings of well-being. The arousal of anger reactions can be controlled by the presence of calm, well-controlled adults.

It is often necessary to offer constructive criticism to a child, but he should not be reminded constantly of his display of angry behavior. A child needs to be denied many things. With the denial should go constructive suggestions concerning things that he can have or do that he will enjoy and that are good for him.

There are times when a child may be justified in his anger. Consciously or unconsciously, an adult may be responsible for the situation which rightly arouses the child to a display of anger. Hence, the anger-arousing situation should be understood by both the adult and the child if the display of anger is to be controlled. Praise or approval is effective in helping a child to overcome resentment of a real or an imaginary hurt. Attempts to quiet a child by reasoning often increase anger rather than alleviate it.

Value of Anger. Anger sometimes has positive values. It can be used to overcome fear, as has been demonstrated in the behavior of men on the battlefield. Some persons cannot get started on a project until they are sufficiently aroused or become indignant at injustices that exist. Any violent anger, however, usually causes a child or older person to dissipate his energies. Anger can serve an individual in a time of crisis by giving him enough added strength to pull him through a difficult situation.

Jealousy. The combining of the feelings of subjugation and inferiority with fear, anger, and affection causes the arousal of the emotional state commonly referred to as jealousy.

Nature of Jealousy. Jealousy concerns itself with the loss or fear of loss of desired affection, or of other goals in which the individual is intensely interested. The prospect of loss arouses anger since an individual's pride and self-esteem may be shattered. Jealousy represents an attitude of resentment which generally centers around other people.

When other persons, objects, or conditions actually or seemingly deny to the child or older person the affection, honor, or position which he desires for himself, jealous behavior is likely to be the result. Sometimes jealousy expresses itself in direct attack, but it is more likely to be exhibited through subtle and indirect behavior.

In most instances of jealousy the anger response is present. There is an impulse to attack, to sulk, or to become vengeful. Also implicit in jealousy are fear responses, often including feelings of

70

inferiority in the situation. Each of these has particular significance as it relates to the important and dominant force of affection for a coveted person, object, or ideal. The jealous response may take possession of the individual's thoughts or it may be sporadic. In other words, it may become a kind of obsession or it may be aroused only when the individual is confronted directly by the jealousy-producing conditions.

Jealousy is born in social settings. In the home the parents are usually responsible for the arousal of jealousy in the child. The child, for example, has been the center of attention in the home, but when another child is born the situation changes. Although the older child still craves the attention and affection of his parents, the new baby may be given more than his share of the mother's time and attention. Age differences of eighteen months or more appear to produce relatively little expression of jealousy, however.

In a young child, jealousy may take the form of injury to the offender, bed-wetting, pretense of illness, refusal to eat, sucking of thumb, or ignoring of the offender. In older children, quarreling, teasing, gossiping, boasting, ridicule, and the use of sarcasm are common ways of exhibiting jealous behavior. Each child utilizes the method that gives him the greatest satisfaction.

In the home or outside the home, any real or imagined signs of discrimination in the amount of attention given to children may cause the child who believes himself to be discriminated against to become jealous. He then uses compensating behavior to call attention to himself, such as loud speech or other forms of aggressive behavior. Oversolicitous mothers or nagging mothers have a high percentage of jealous children.

Control of Jealousy. One way of preventing a child's developing a jealous attitude toward a newborn baby in the family would be to give to the older child for his use any gifts brought by friends for the new baby. The latter, of course, cannot use toys, for example, that may be brought, but the older child can enjoy them. The sibling then may be glad that the baby has arrived since his coming has been rewarding.

To avoid any display of jealousy on the part of a child is almost impossible. Even though siblings may be treated in exactly the same way by parents who consciously attempt to show no discrimination in their behavior, no two children are alike in their reactions.

Hence, one or another of the children soon comes to recognize that he may be inferior in one or another way to his brothers or sisters. This arouses a fear that his own inadequacy may deny him what the others should or do receive in the way of attention. Resentments develop which may lead to feelings of jealousy.

The pride of possession is deep-seated and is a fundamental factor in the arousal of jealousy. As the child's interests carry him outside the family, he may become less concerned about family conditions and situations. Hence, he may lose his more obvious symptoms of jealousy. Unless fairness and objectivity have been characteristic of relationships in the home, however, the child may develop a habitual jealous attitude that affects his relationship with other people throughout his life.

Fear and Worry. Emotional states born of feelings of insecurity usually represent the bases of serious maladjustment. No matter what the age of a person is, he needs to be reasonably secure in relations with other people and in ability to handle situations and conditions that constitute his day-by-day life pattern. Otherwise, he may retreat from what can be considered normal activity. If the fear and worry become too intense, the individual may lose contact with reality.

Fear — Its Causes and Expression. Children are susceptible to the arousal of fears that may be real or imaginary. Fear-arousing stimuli vary widely in their form and in their effect upon the developing child. What to the secure child may be just one of his many new experiences may to another young person constitute an intolerable situation from which he feels himself driven to retreat.

The infant's accustomed responses to loud noises, loss of support, or falling a short distance are clutching movements, and whimpering and crying. The young child who has been sheltered unduly in the home may give evidence of his fears of the unknown by shyness in the presence of strangers, or by complete withdrawal from unaccustomed situations.

A child tends to reflect the fears of his edlers. In the adult, the fear of a situation may be relatively mild but, as he gives evidence that the fear does exist, he may arouse in the child an unreasonable fear of a situation. It is in this manner that many childhood fears are developed, such as fear of storms, closed places, high places, death, teachers, or novel situations.

An adult may say, more or less casually, in the presence of a child, for example, "I am scared to death of thunder and lightning." The adult does not mean this statement literally, but to the child its connotation is clear — death, which he may have just come to recognize as a dire calamity, will result from a storm. The child tends to fear a situation that threatens his safety or security. Hence, the adult's idle remark may arouse an intense fear which may persist for a long time or until the child has had many experiences with storms that have not had fatal results.

The more imaginative the child is and the less experience he has in out-going play activities with peer groups, the more sensitive he is to possible fear-producing stimuli. Darkness, unusual sounds, and similar situations and conditions may so stimulate his imagination that he becomes lost in a mental world peopled by hobgoblins, robbers, ghosts, and other "supernatural" agents of evil or harm to himself. He may be in constant dread of the loss of a beloved parent or friend, of an accident, or of personal ineffectiveness.

A feeling of inadequacy and consequent fear reactions may be especially noticeable in a child who leaves home for school, and who associates with many different people outside the home, unless he has been prepared gradually by his parents for entrance into this new and larger world. He may develop fear of his teacher, of his schoolmates who appear to be better adjusted than himself, or of failure in class activities. It is only as he is helped to find a place for himself in his new environment that these fears can be successfully overcome.

Phobias. Phobias are pathological fears and, under certain circumstances, can be developed easily. They are symbolic but may affect a person throughout his life. These morbid, irrational fears can be aroused by any one of many situations, such as a closed road, high places, or crowds. An individual who has developed a phobia often is unable to explain his feelings or the cause of the phobia. He tries to conceal from his associates the persistent fear that tends to influence his behavior in situations that arouse his abnormal emotional state.

The symbolic origin of phobias has led to many attempts on the part of psychologists to explain these irrational fears. Some attribute the phobia to the experiencing of guilt feelings arising from either real or imagined sex behavior that is socially disapproved.

It is difficult to eliminate a phobia after it has developed. A very pleasant stimulus may help to eradicate a phobia if that stimulus is associated with the supposed fear situation. The introduction of strong anger-arousing stimuli into the situation may afford temporary relief.

Worry. Worry is not aroused by any direct stimulus such as is found in the child's immediate physical environment, but rather arises out of an imagined fear of a possible unpleasant experience. Hence, worry is not found among very young children. The child must have matured sufficiently in his mental abilities for him to imagine things not immediately present in order that he may be capable of worrying.

Worry affects everyone to one degree or another. It deals with a past experience or with something that may happen in the future about which nothing is being done at present. If the circumstance that causes it is removed, the worry disappears. The child experiences worry if or when he develops an attitude of inferiority or a feeling of personal inadequacy or futility, or if he believes that he lacks preparation for the solution of a problem with which he is faced. Worry results from the dread of meeting situations for which the child or older person feels unprepared. It represents a kind of imaginary fear of things that probably never materialize.

The adolescent worries about many things. He realizes that he no longer is a child. However, no matter how strongly he asserts that he is nearing adulthood and should be so treated, he recognizes his own actual or potential inadequacies. He wants independence but feels himself to be unable to make decisions or to act for himself. Hence, he worries about his appearance, the correctness of his dress and manners, the attitude of his peers toward himself, his chances of social and vocational success. For some adolescents, life consists of one worry followed by another. The more emotionalized the young person becomes over possible undesirable eventualities, the more aggressive his behavior may seem to be, unless his disturbed state becomes so intense that he attempts to retreat from all the situations that are becoming intolerable to him.

Constructive Attitudes Toward Fear and Worry. Although the elimination of fear is difficult, it is important that a child be helped to rid himself of as many unnecessary fears as possible. To do this, one must understand the nature of the situation in which the fear arises.

Every child should master those fear situations that will assist him to become cautious for his own good and the good of others. He should be aware of the danger of being hit by a car when he is

74

crossing the street; he should be trained not to play with matches lest he start a fire; he should learn that he must not misbehave because by doing so he may lose the approval of his associates.

When correct information is lacking, children tend to respond to situations on an emotional level. It, therefore, is relatively easy to thrill them, since the *unknown* factor is significant in fear-arousing situations. Hence, as many fear-arousing stimuli as possible should be removed from the environment of the growing child. There is doubtful value in attempts to eliminate a child's fears by forcing him to meet a fear situation.

A child cannot be talked out of his fears; nor will adult ridicule of his fear help him overcome it. Trying to reason with the child, in and of itself, will not eliminate fear. To show by personal example that the fear is unfounded may or may not meet with success. The development of certain skills often aids in preventing and overcoming unreasonable fears. In a time of crisis, the display of calmness by those around the child will alleviate some of his tensions. Successful achievement and enjoyable activity have positive tension-reducing value.

Worry is overcome to the extent that a child or an adult engages in meaningful activity which diverts his attention from the cause of the worry. If the worry state arises out of an actual problem situation, an attitude of willingness to meet and solve the problem is helpful. An individual's worry can be alleviated or eliminated if he: (1) thinks through a possible solution to the problem; (2) gathers considerable data that may bear on the solution of the problem; (3) faces the worry, evaluates its cause, and removes that cause if possible; and (4) co-operates with other people in the avoidance or elimination of serious, worry-arousing situations.

No matter how disturbing fear may be at times, it remains an important and desirable human experience unless it takes on the characteristics of a phobia. A certain amount of fear is necessary for protection from harmful elements in the environment. When a child's behavior is so conditioned that he becomes cautious, it is probable that fear of consequences is basic to the development of his cautious attitude. Failure and disaster have been avoided or prevented through such conditioning.

The effects of socializing influences upon a child show themselves in his developing fear of loss of prestige or loss of recognition of his capabilities or achievements. Interpreted in this way, fear may serve as a spur to greater activity. To be motivated to do well or to be well liked indicates a positive, wholesome attitude based upon fear components.

A child should not exhibit so great self-confidence that he appears to be self-centered or aggressive. He should not become timid because of too rigid adult control, but an attitude of too great permissiveness may be harmful to the child.

Anxiety. Basically, fear and anxiety are similar in that both are aroused by some recognition of elements of danger to oneself. They differ, however, in that in fear there is a more or less clearly perceived cause for the aroused emotional state, but anxiety is associated with a feeling of uneasiness instigated by circumstances that the individual is unable to define objectively. The emotional reaction tends to be vague or diffused. Something is threatening a person but he is not quite certain what it is.

In a particular situation, the victim of anxiety is likely to say to himself, "Something is likely to happen. I don't know what it is, but I'm worried about it." A mother, for example, is anxious about the safe return home of her seven-year-old child who has gone to the neighbor to visit. When the child's return home is delayed beyond the time set for her return, the mother's anxiety becomes intensified. If she cannot do anything positive about it the mother might develop a severe headache or other ailment, which disappears when the daughter arrives.

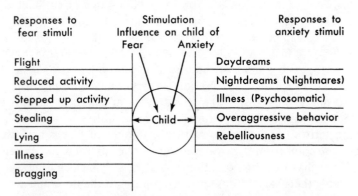

Responses to fear stimuli	Stimulation Influence on child of Fear Anxiety	Responses to anxiety stimuli
Flight		Daydreams
Reduced activity		Nightdreams (Nightmares)
Stepped up activity		Illness (Psychosomatic)
Stealing	←Child→	Overaggressive behavior
Lying		Rebelliousness
Illness		
Bragging		

Some Ways a Child Responds to Fear-Producing Stimuli and to Anxiety-Producing Stimuli

The form in which anxiety shows itself differs among individuals. Some children seem almost unconsciously to enjoy being anxious about something. Inner conflict may cause a child to seek the kind of situation in which his anxious state is rooted. a preadolescent may be concerned about his prestige in his group. He may experience a vague anxiety that he may do or say something that might harm his self-esteem. His chief worries are in the area of home relationships, school activities and social relationships among his peers.

CHAPTER 7

Development of Meaning and Understanding

The study of a child's developing mental, emotional, and language patterns of behavior includes some consideration of the development of his power to understand and to put meaning into his life experiences. There is, however, a continuity of progression apparent in this aspect of development that requires separate treatment, although all other phases of growth and development are basic to it and closely associated with its progress.

THE BASES OF UNDERSTANDING

Whether the child, during his prenatal or neonatal stages of development, possesses to even slight degree any of what can be termed consciousness, or awareness and understanding, is open to controversy. It can be stated, however, that during the fetal stage are being formed all the prerequisites for mental activity that can be expected to be developed soon after birth.

Components of Understanding. The development of understanding involves the putting of meaning into all the environmental aspects of life or the building of concepts concerning elements within and outside oneself and one's relation to these elements. It represents a progressive pattern of development that requires adequate functioning of the nervous system. Physical factors make possible the experiencing of sensations and the formation of percepts that then can be translated into concepts.

Relation between Sensation and Perception. A sensation can be defined roughly as an individual's first, unlearned response to any factor of his environment that stimulates the activity of a particular sense organ. As one sensation is associated with another, the interaction between the central nervous system and the sensory impulse leads to an interpreation of the sensory response. This reaction can be regarded as perception, or the attaching of meaning to the sensation.

It is probable that only a very young child experiences pure sensation. The first time he is affected by a stimulus from within or without himself his response is generally automatic. A feeling of discomfort or of hunger, a loud noise, or a bright light brings on an appropriate response without the infant's awareness of the meaning of the sensation in relation to himself. Gradually, however, he begins to make simple associations between experienced sensations and their significance to him. He is learning to perceive. As new sensory stimuli affect the child, he comes to perceive that each new experience is different from former ones. The recognition of the newness of the experience is a form of perception.

As the number of different percepts of a particular object, condition, or situation increases, a general meaning, usually in the form of a word or phrase, is attached to this combination of percepts. This general meaning can then be carried over for the purpose of identification to other situations in which similar objects or conditions exist. The individual now can be said to have gained a more or less adequate conceptual understanding of one or another phenomenon.

What actually takes place within the central nervous system during this process is not yet known. Nevertheless, studies of the relationship of sensation and perception to the development of understanding have yielded some knowledge of the developmental sequence.

BEGINNINGS OF SENSORY DEVELOPMENT

All an individual's knowledge and understanding of the world in which he lives is gained through the functioning of his various sense organs, such as visual, auditory, tactile, heat, cold, pain, olfactory, gustatory, kinesthetic, and organic. The degree to which each of these senses functions adequately at the various stages of his development is basic to his progressing power of understanding.

Prenatal and Neonatal Responses. At birth, the neonate possesses all his sense organs, which have achieved a fair degree of

79

growth during the fetal stage. Some of them even function in a feeble way during the prebirth period. During the first weeks of life the infant seems to respond to light. This fact can be observed as he turns his eyes toward a light and seems to be disturbed by an intense light. Objects around him apparently have no meaning for him. It is only gradually that he becomes aware of them and, through repeated experiences, can differentiate among them in a general way.

It is not known how much the infant can hear, although he may respond to loud sounds by changes in bodily movements and respiration. During this early period, he seems to "like" the taste of sweet solutions and to be discouraged by salt solutions. With further development comes a more definite reaction for or against relatively strong substances, but the infant does not seem able to distinguish among milder flavors.

The neonate is sensitive to heat and cold, hunger and thirst, and pain and pressure. He responds to these sensory stimuli with expressed feelings of pleasantness and unpleasantness. His feeling state can be recognized by changes in his bodily movements and facial expression, and by his smiling or crying. At first these responses are diffused and seem to affect the entire body. Gradually, the baby learns to distinguish among sensations, and his responses become more definite and localized. He is putting meaning into his sensations. The beginnings of perception are present.

Later Responses. With increase in maturation and diversity of environmental stimulation, the child not only gains greater sensory acuity but also improves his responses to stimuli. The child begins to understand what his mother means in relation to himself when she says "No! No!" with a shake of her head, or calls him a good baby while she pats him. He recognizes the differences in his mother's or nurse's handling of him and that of another person who is not accustomed to holding babies.

Other more definite and meaningful reactions come to be experienced. For example, as a result of past pleasant experiences with it he reaches for his orange juice and drinks it with satisfaction. He may repeat the word "juice" or make sounds that approximate the word when his mother offers it to him with the comment, "Here is your orange juice." It is much later, though, before he is able to make a connection between the whole orange which his mother cuts and squeezes in his presence and the juice which he drinks. Even then, at first, his understanding may seem to be confused. He may point to a whole orange and attempt to say "juice." The differentiation between the orange and the juice comes only when he has had the oft-repeated experience of watching his mother extract the juice and then offer it to him.

All a child's sensations need to be built and refined through constant and continuing experiences with them. It sometimes is difficult for an adult to realize that to the young child the adult's world of accustomed sensory stimulation constitutes a mass of new stimuli to which the child can respond only in terms of the maturational stage of his sense organs.

DEVELOPMENT OF PERCEPTS

By the age of three the child has progressed far toward his maximum of sensory acuity. Along with the increased sensory acuity goes similar progress toward the building of meaning into his experiences.

Since a percept can be thought of as a meaningful sensation, it is important that the child be provided with experiences that present clear and appropriate sensory material. The young child, for example, has not yet had sufficient experience to recognize the meaning of a suggestion or command that is mumbled or expressed in terms with which he has had no experience. He must be helped to interpret such material correctly. A vague or inaccurately interpreted sensation will result in incomplete, faulty, or incorrect associations.

Factors of Perception. The quality and extent of a child's perceptions are influenced by the acuity of his sense organs, the amount and kind of stimulation to which he is exposed, his past experience, his interests, and his degree of attention to the stimulating situation. The interests of a child usually are fleeting, and his attention span is short. Consequently, his first percepts are likely to consist of general outlines. It is only as his experiences increase and his interest is stimulated that he shifts his attention from the whole to one or more details of an object that have come to have meaning for him.

In this respect the perception of a child differs from that of an adult. The attention span of adults is longer than that of a child, and their interests are more stable. Consequently, an adult is able to "take in" more of the significant elements of an object or situation than can a child. In response to stimuli, a child has much to learn before he assigns the same meaning to a sound or other sensory stimulus that adults have learned to take for granted. To an adult a sound may mean danger, but in a child it may arouse only a response of delight, until or unless his experience with that particular sound changes his understanding of it.

Progress in Perception. A child's early percepts are concerned chiefly with elements that are of immediate interest or value to himself. He perceives that some objects move, some can be eaten, others make sounds, and still others give off light. He later puts specific meaning into his perceptions. He recognizes a moving object as his father's foot. The light may be coming through the window or from a lighted object (a lamp) in the room. He distinguishes various foods set before him by their general form, color, or other characteristics. He may make mistakes, however, either because of his lack of attention to detail or as a result of his interest or mental set at the moment. He sees what to him appears to be ice cream. As a result of former pleasant experiences with ice cream, he wants some. When he tastes the cottage cheese which he has interpreted wrongly, he discovers his mistakes and recognizes the fact that everything is not what it seems to be. He must observe more carefully the next time.

Illusions. Faulty perception occurs frequently not only in the life of a child but also in that of an adult. Errors of perception usually are referred to as *illusions.* The errors have their bases in various factors mentioned earlier: poorly functioning sense organs, inadequate stimulation of the sense organs, or mental set. If any one or more of these factors is distorted the individual cannot form correct impressions. Incorrect interpretation may be associated with any of the sense organs, but it is most common in sight and hearing.

Illusions are possible concerning objects at a considerable distance, the size of objects, the color of objects, or objects in motion. A train may appear to move backwards, the rails of the railroad track may seem to converge, bridge posts may disappear if they are passed at a rapid speed, or rotating spokes of wheels may seem to rotate backwards if they are observed through a picket fence. These are common examples of the many illusions that may be experienced daily and are normal for both children and adults.

Refinement of Perception. At first, children perceive only what is present to their senses. They are unable to interpret their sensory experiences in such a way as to recognize more or less subtle meanings. Studies of children's interpretation of pictures indicate that the child first recognizes or perceives objects in the picture that are known to him, especially those in which he is interested or with which he has had one or another kind of experience. Later, he is able to perceive activity, which, however, again is interpreted in terms of his more or less immediate interest or experience.

It is only when he becomes relatively mature that he is able to divorce his interpretation of sensed material from his personal interests or activities. The personal factor continues to influence the individual's interpretation of whatever he perceives. One sign of social maturity, however, is the ability of the developing child or adult to combine personal and social factors in his interpretation of his life experiences. The extent to which an individual is in the process of refining or has refined his perceptive powers can be discovered through the administration of thematic apperception tests, in which the subject is asked what is happening in a picture. The subject's responses throw considerable light upon the thought processes of the child, especially in the later stages of his development.

Sex Differences. According to some studies, girls tend to perceive objects as a whole, whereas boys appear to excel girls in perceiving what to them are utilization of the Rorschach or "ink-blot" interpretation technique, give evidence of the superiority of girls of elementary school age over boys during the same age in ability to note details and in maturity of response to form and color.

Individual Differences. Children differ in the rate at which they recognize perceptual relationships. The child of superior mental ability and sensory acuity may surprise adults by his relatively mature understanding of environmental elements in relation to one another. Contrariwise, a slow developer may have difficulty in recognizing even the simplest relationships. As in other areas of development, a child may seem unaware of his surroundings during his early years and then exhibit unexpected power of perception.

A child who suffers from one or another sensory defect may need to achieve his percepts through greater utilization of those sensory organs that are functioning normally. It is probable, however, that such a child's percepts will be different from those of children whose sense organs are generally adequate. Meager or rich environmental stimulations also affect the extent to which a child is able to establish enriched perception. Differences among children

83

resulting from differences in home background are especially noticeable in the first year of school life. In general, however, most children follow a more or less uniform sequential pattern of growing awareness and understanding.

DEVELOPMENT OF CONCEPTS

Sensation, perception, and the consequent building of generalized and specific ideas of objects, conditions, and situations are so closely related that it is almost impossible to treat them separately.

Meaning of Concepts. A concept can be regarded as a generalized meaning expressed in a symbol (usually a word or phrase) that represents relationships in experience. Hence, through many percepts and their inner associations, the child gradually builds up meanings for the words and phrases that, at successive stages of his development, constitute his language pattern. Understanding becomes more effective as the child's vocabulary increases. Finer discriminations are made among the symbols or words at his disposal, as a result of greater and more differentiated experience.

A child's first concepts must of necessity be simple because of the immaturity of his growing nervous and sensory systems. Hence, too great stimulation of his sensory organs or too varied an interpretation of a sensation or combination of sensations is likely to result in a confused or inaccurate concept by the child. For example, in his daily experiences, the child has come to know a *cup* as something into which his milk is poured. He probably also has had experience with *butter* as something that is put on bread to make it taste good. Then he is introduced to the new word sound *buttercup*. In the light of his experience, a buttercup must be a cup into which one puts butter. Unless, as he hears the word, he also sees the flower and has the reason for its name explained to him, he is making the only association possible for him. It may take a long time for the child to appreciate the falsity of his understanding of this word unless he chances to see a buttercup itself or a picture of it. During the child's early (and perhaps even later) struggles to perceive and to understand his expanding world, many such false concepts may be experienced. Some of these persist into and event through adult life.

A word or phrase represents a real experience, but it is an abstraction to the extent that it connotes certain characteristics that are common to the kind of object, condition or situation, or idea which it symbolizes. Complete understanding of the symbol is acquired only through accurate perception that gradually is refined and enlarged to the point where it can be embodied in a relatively correct, meaningful symbol. Unless the child experiences adequate perceptions, he is likely to amass a number of symbols (words or phrases) which he can repeat by rote but which do not represent meaningful concepts. When this happens, a child may acquire a great deal of faulty or false information that may lead to the building of inadequate or erroneous concepts or ideas concerning either his inner or his outer life.

Factors in Conceptual Development. Accepting the thesis that the development of concepts is dependent upon sensory and perceptual experiences, other aspects of developing behavior also must be considered.

Interest and Attention. The attention span of the child for interesting activity increases from about six seconds at the age of two to about thirteen seconds at the age of five. It can be expected, therefore, that he will become increasingly able to concentrate upon one object for an increasingly longer period. He also will be able to attend to more complex situations or to specific aspects of a total situation.

The duration and span of a growing child's attention usually are influenced by his immediate interest and his physical condition. Other factors include the kind and amount of motivation utilized to focus his attention on a particular object or a particular situation, and the complexity of the object or situation in relation to his stage of maturation.

Motor Co-ordination. The development in the child of motor co-ordination to the extent that he thereby is enabled to grasp and hold objects is another factor of progress in conceptual learning. As he grasps, holds, and manipulates objects he becomes aware of certain qualities that cannot be perceived through the eye or ear. These qualities include smoothness, roughness, hardness, and softness. Tactual experiences do not become a part of a child's conceptual life, however, until he can associate the feel with its proper symbol or descriptive word.

Children's Questions. Another way in which children gain an understanding of their surroundings is through the questions they ask. The so-called questioning period begins at about the third year and continues unabatedly until about the sixth year, when the child usually enters the elementary school. The kind and amount of social pressure which he then experiences affect the extent to which he continues to ask questions and the value to himself of this method of obtaining information.

The kinds of questions that young children ask, according to studies in the field, usually begin with the *what* and *where* questions. Although these types of questions are continued, other forms begin. By the time the child is about four years old, he begins to ask questions that deal with the *how, why,* and *when* of things. Answers to these questions need to be simple in form. The adult who attempts to give information to young children should keep in mind that the child's background of experience is limited. Therefore, extraneous factors or interpretations that go beyond the child's power to assimilate should be avoided.

With increasing maturity, the child's questions tend to be less related to immediate happenings and concrete materials, and to become more concerned with relatively abstract relationships and more remote and impersonal matters. As soon as he can read with some facility, he is likely to seek the answers to his questions from books as much as from other persons, if not more so.

Concept of Self. By the time the child is six months old he has begun to give evidence of having formed some more or less definite concepts about himself. He is not able to verbalize these. He handles his body and looks at himself in the mirror. He tries to get his fingers and toes into his mouth and pulls at his nose and ears. When he is able to enunciate words like "baby," he seems to derive great satisfaction from being held close to a mirror. As he looks at his reflection he seems to be admiring himself and attempts to pat his reflection. He also may smile and continue to repeat "Baby" or "Nice baby."

He also can be taught to identify, by pointing to them, his eyes, nose, mouth, ears, and toes. By the time he is about two and one-half years old he should be able to point out the hair, mouth, ears, and hands on a large paper doll. According to Terman, the three-year-old child should know his first and last name and whether he is a boy or girl.

Many children between the ages of three and four know a great deal about themselves, are much interested in themselves, and may be much concerned about their clothes and their general appearance. Little girls, especially, want to wear their mothers' shoes, smear their faces with lipstick and face powder, and then admire themselves in the mirror or demand the admiration of adults.

The child's recognition of himself as an individual, apart from adults and other children, certainly is present at the age of four years and may have been achieved earlier. By this time he probably has developed two concepts of himself. One of these can be described as more or less objective, and concerns his body and appearance and what he can do as compared with other children. The other self is related to all his inner feelings, attitudes, and thoughts. The second self is not easily observed by others except as his inner life shows itself in his behavior.

During childhood, this dichotomy between the objective and the subjective selves may lead to confusion within the child. He is uncertain as to which self is really *himself.* His dream world and his real world sometimes become so interwoven that adults find him unpredictable and difficult to understand. It is only as he matures and changes gradually from an egocentric to a more social being that he can begin to merge the two selves.

Orientation to Space. Orientation in space relationships is an important aspect of perceptual and conceptual development that may lead to confusion on the part of the average child. As a baby, he learns to say "up" and to stretch up his arms when he wishes to be taken from his crib. This is a more or less mechanical response based upon imitative behavior. The understanding of differences between *up* and *down, right* and *left, before* and *behind,* or *above* and *below* comes slowly and only after much experience with the differences themselves and their correct terminology.

For the child who spends most of his preschool time in the home or in its immediate environs, places remote from his accustomed habitat mean nothing to him. He gets lost if he attempts to leave his house or block. The six-year-old may have to be escorted to school even though the school may be very close to his home. As soon as he can find his own way, however, he tends to resent an adult's accompanying him.

Gradually, the child acquires some understanding of the fact that there are interesting places removed from his home and neighborhood environment. This is especially so if, as a younger child, he has experienced the taking of trips with his parents. Although he acquires a concept of a place as being *away* from home, he has relatively little understanding of how much that "awayness" may be.

The understanding of distance in terms of the number of blocks from one place to another comes only with experience. The concept may be a verbal one. The child learns, perhaps, that a block is a part of a street, but the walking of two blocks may seem to be hundreds of blocks, especially if he is tired. His concepts of various linear measurements usually begin in terms of home experiences. The length of a foot at first may mean the length of his father's foot; a yard may mean the space between his mother's nose and the hand of her extended arm. It is not until he is introduced to a ruler in school that he gains what can be considered to be a satisfactory concept of an inch, a foot, or a yard. Even then the child (and sometimes the older person) has difficulty in marking off a linear unit on paper in terms of his concept of it. A mile has little meaning for a child until he reaches high school age or later, except that he may have a verbal concept of a mile as twenty blocks, regardless of the length of the blocks themselves.

Orientation to Time. Another important area of conceptual development is that of orientation in time. The young child lives in the present. *Yesterday* and *tomorrow* are vague terms used by adults that mean little or nothing to him until he reaches the age of three or later. Even then, tomorrow or this afternoon is thought of as *not now but after now*. He gradually comes to understand that sleep separates *now* from *then*. Yesterday is before he went to sleep, and tomorrow is when he awakens. For example, a three-year old was promised that the family would have a picnic in the country "tomorrow." After his afternoon nap, he exclaimed, "It's tomorrow — let's go to picnic."

Before the child starts to go to school, he may have learned to repeat the names of the days of the week, but even the six-year-old has difficulty in remembering the names and is unsure of their sequence. It is not until he is seven that he gains an accurate understanding of which month it is. He is eight before he can name the months and give the day of the month.

"Telling time" is difficult for the average child. He must be helped to develop this ability through patient attempts on the part of an adult to familiarize the child with the hands of the clock and their significance in different positions. Larger time units and time relationships may not be understood accurately by the child until he is twelve years old or older. Approximation of time units is difficult for some people at any age. To ask the members of an adult group to guess the passage of time during a minute by the clock often yields interesting results.

Form and Color Concepts. The development of form and color concepts begins early. If asked, for example, to match two objects out of three on the basis of either form or color, a child under three years of age tends to match on the basis of form; from three to six years of age he matches in terms of color; from the age of six onward matching usually again is done on the basis of form. This type of experience finds its counterpart in the daily life of the growing child. At first, people or objects are differentiated in terms of general form similarities. All women are "mommy," and all men are "daddy." Anything round is a ball, and any flower may be a rose.

A little later, the child becomes intensely interested in color differences. In picking out animals in his picture book, he is likely to emphasize the color of different animals as a *black* doggy, a *red* cow. By kindergarten age he may make his choices relatively in terms of intensity of color or largeness of size. Not only do children respond to bright color early, but also they give evidence of steadily increasing ability to discriminate among colors, although they are more discriminating in the matter of hues (red, blue, yellow, etc.) than they are in differences in saturation or brightness.

There is some relationship between a child's developing understanding of form and color and his appreciation of space differences. As a young child, he may recognize the fact that the big chair is over there but that his little chair is here. If he spends his early years in a house that has two floors he learns to know, especially after he has developed the power of walking, that he goes to sleep in his bed upstairs. Gradually the child can place his play toys in space. Some children acquire the ability by the time they are three years old or even younger to put their toys away after they have finished playing. At first the toys may be thrown into a closet, drawer, or other receptable in a more or less disordered fashion. Before long, however, the child appears to achieve some understanding of object-space relationships and can arrange his toys with some regard to relative size and available space.

Number Concepts. Children acquire general concepts of *muchness, moreness, bigness,* and *littleness* relatively early. The child who has begun to use words is likely to demand, "more, more" of candy which he likes, when he has finished eating his food, he may say "No more," or "A-gone" (all gone), while he points to his empty dish. The use of the word symbols probably results from his imitation of adult speech. He appears, however, to have some understanding of the meaning of the words.

The young child apparently has some understanding of gross relationships. The baby may stretch his arms above his head while he says, "Baby so big." During the nursery school period, the child can be trained to take one, two, or three crackers with his milk. Although a relatively young child can be taught to count from one to ten, there is little evidence that he has any functional or coordinated concepts of what is meant by these numbers. Such understanding comes later as a result of systematic training in number discrimination.

DEVELOPMENT OF REASONING

Lack of experience is a deterrent to the child's development of the power to recognize relationships among the various elements of his environment or to make needed associations for adequate understanding of cause-and-effect relationships.

Understanding Cause and Effect. Young children probably have some understanding of simple situations long before they are able to express their understanding verbally. Even the young child appears to know that throwing his rattle or other toy on the floor may bring a disapproving reaction from his mother. He learns early to act in one way in the presence of one adult and in a different way for another adult. He seems able to vary his behavior in terms of expected adult reactions to it.

From the age of two to four, the child gives evidence in his behavior that he is able to make simple generalizations in relation to objects and people about him. His thinking is on a plane that is much different from that of adults. Consequently, his behavior based upon his maturational stage of mental development may earn adult disapproval. This fact may astonish him, for he may think that he did exactly what was expected of him. In his childish way he may even reason that there is no satisfying these hard-to-please grown-ups.

Progress in Reasoning Ability. The reasoning process of the child at the age of six is the same as it is at the age of twelve or later. He can draw a childish but to himself adequate conclusion concerning a group of objects in his environment with which he has had

90

experience. As he makes his generalization he is more or less following the adult's pattern of reasoning. He also is able to reason from a generalization to specific instances, again in his childish fashion. His mother tells him to be good. To him that means that he can do this or that he also achieves increased ability to solve a variety of problems, although the explanations which he gives for his solutions are not always consistent.

The child's behavior in trying to solve a problem is not unlike that of adults when they are dealing with unfamiliar material, but his general experiential background and his lack of facility in combining elements of a problem reflect immaturity. Often, when he attempts to solve a problem, the form in which the problem is thought of by him or stated to him by another may not be entirely clear to him. The significance of the inferences inherent in the problem may not be recognized. His attempts at solution are thus hampered by inadequate understanding or misunderstanding of the problem situation, as well as by the fact that he may apply experiences that to him are more or less verbal concepts. Consequently, his generalization or conclusion is apt to be erroneous.

Growth in Reasoning and Problem Solving. The young child's lack of experience causes his reasoning or attempts at solving a problem to seem to the child to be erroneous or even far-fetched. Early in life the child gains some idea of cause and effect relationships. He discovers that to touch or handle some objects or to throw things on the floor receives adult disapproval. Hence he associates parental frowns, the slapping of his little hands, or other forms of punishment with his engaging in this or that wrong action. The child becomes confused, however, if certain acts which seem to him no different from others which he performs are greeted with smiles of approbation while others receive disapproval.

Another deterrent to a child's building definite cause-and-effect relationships is fostered by difference in attitude between his parents. For example, his father may ignore or actually encourage behavior which is disapproved by his mother. Hence he learns that cause and effect vary with people. Because of his immaturity, the child often cannot comprehend all the implications of the raw materials which he is attempting to manipulate. He may not recognize the significant inferences inherent in the problem. Inadequate understanding of the problem causes him to evolve erroneous conclusions.

Between the ages of seven and eleven, the child begins to engage in logical thinking. Although he is still somewhat self-centered, he is able to get outside himself and recognize cause-and-effect relationships in the world about him. Natural phenomena take on an added meaning. The seasons of the year become real concepts, representing weather and temperature changes. Yet the seasons may be identified more definitely in light of personal interests: Summer means vacation from school; Winter brings the Christmas gifts and fun. Boys, especially, tend to associate the seasons with different kinds of sports. Many childish evaluations of things and conditions continue through much of the experiences of others.

During later childhood, the young person is likely to be extremely curious about his world. He is intrigued by all the different people and things that stimulate his senses. He wants to experiment and, through his experiences, build new and satisfying concepts. He looks for cause-and-effect relationships and enjoys solving problems that arise in his daily life. Previous experiences still tend to affect the accuracy of his conclusions, however. He gains much satisfaction from comparing his thoughts and feelings with those of his peers.

Immaturity in conceptual thinking and reasoning is commonly evidenced by older elementary school children when they attempt to solve percentage problems in arithmetic that involve, for example, profit and loss, discounts, or interest on money invested. Such problems may be difficult for the child whose concepts are more or less verbal. First, he may not fully understand the meaning of the important terms included in the statement of the problem. Second, he may attempt to apply a formula in its solution which he has learned by rote but which he does not understand. Consequently, he may apply the wrong formula, which may yield fantastic results. He may not recognize the impossibility of his answer because of his immature concept of relationships.

CHAPTER 8

Creative Activity and Play of Children

As the child gradually acquires percepts and concepts, and gains manipulatory skill, he seems to have an urge to change things in his environment or to enlarge upon what to the adult is the truth of a situation. The young child is highly imaginative. He attempts to take his play toy apart and put it together again in another form. In his recounting of incidents he may so distort or exaggerate them that they are scarcely recognizable.

The apparent destruction of toys and the telling of so-called tall stories represent the beginning of the development of the young person's imagination. The child needs to learn that he should not destroy and that he must be truthful. The fundamental powers of reconstruction or reorganization of emotions can be guided in such ways that eventually he may be able to use his imaginative powers. He is motivated to create something that is truly original and constructive.

IMAGINATION IN CREATIVE ACTIVITY

Imagination plays an influential role in a child's mental and emotional life. Through it he gains experience with things beyond his actual reach. He projects his wants and desires well beyond the bounds of reality. He makes use of imagination in his associations with other children, especially as he engages in make-believe activities.

Role of Make-believe. The early life of a child is full of situations in which make-believe plays an important role. Make-believe activities serve numerous functions in his mental life. He can play free-and-easy with reality. He can make it conform to his mental restrictions when it suits his fancy, since he does not have sufficient data to construct realistic ideas. He permits himself to manipulate ideas even though he only partly grasps them, and he can solve problems without the necessity of utilizing all relevant data.

The young child can create and re-create situations, and plan extensive programs of activity. The little girl serves dinner to her dolls. The young boy takes an imaginary trip to see his relatives in several states. These and other make-believe activities associated with the reconstruction of family life in imagination reveal how the child's mind is stimulated toward thinking.

Through make-believe, children may rid themselves of disagreeable situations or of conditions that annoy or thwart them. In this way, imagination helps the child to escape from what to him is an intolerable situation. Imagination sometimes may arouse fear and anxiety as he anticipates an event before it happens or anticipates that which never will happen. As he grows older, experience helps the child to bring his anticipatory imagination into line with what is more likely to be reality.

Make-believe is actively associated with social development. The play of most preschool children is filled with make-believe activities. Thus the bond that pulls these children together is strengthened. The make-believe setting enables children to tolerate each other more easily than would be characteristic of a realistic situation.

Creative activity bounds in settings in which make-believe is present. Displaying polite manners and dressing up in various costumes, accompanied by a parading before an imaginary audience, illustrate the relation of wholesome thinking to make-believe.

Role of Fantasy. Fantasy is a form of make-believe. It is stimulated through the child's experience with nursery rhymes and fairy tales. The child delights in the nursery rhymes that are read to him during his early years. Later, as he achieves the ability to read, he may thrill to the exploits of his favorite fairy-tale heroes and heroines. This attitude continues to be exhibited by the child when he is old enough to watch motion picture and television programs. The boy usually prefers tales of adventure; the girl becomes emotionalized over romantic stories even though she may not comprehend fully their implications.

Nursery rhymes, fairy stories, and other emotion-arousing tales often provide excitement that is well beyond the child's ability to encompass. As he projects himself into situations that are far removed from everyday happenings he is called upon to play dramatic and heroic roles and utilize powers and abilities that lie beyond his real understanding. Overemphasis upon the exploits of a favorite hero or heroine is likely to arouse in him unachievable ambitions about which he dreams rather than to help him live within his own ability and environmental limitations.

The great danger to the young child of engaging in fantasy it that thereby he is encouraged to retreat from the demands of the world of reality. Moreover, the child may tend to carry over into later life the confusion between fact and fancy that he has experienced earlier. If fantasies are casual and not systematic they may have value in that they sharpen his imaginative abilities. As a result he may be stimulated, in adult life, to engage in worth-while and even significant creative activities.

NEED FOR CREATIVE EXPRESSION

It is evident that a child's imagination needs opportunities for expression. In the past, too much emphasis may have been placed by parents and teachers upon the importance of a child's acquiring the knowledges and skills that are accepted as fundamental to successful management of the daily routines of living. It was recognized that the child needed to learn to read and to master the fundamentals of arithmetic. These learnings are essential, but we have come to recognize the equal importance of guiding the development of the child's imagination and his urge to express his interests and his creative abilities through media such as the dance, music, drawing, and imaginative writing.

The Early School Years. At present, the nursery school, kindergarten, and first grade of the elementary school provide many opportunities for the young child to engage in free activity. He is encouraged to give vent to his imagination through drawing, singing, dancing, and story-telling.

Contrary to some former opinions, every child possesses imagination. If properly guided he can create something that to him at least is new and different. His created products may be crude and unrealistic, but they satisfy him, especially during his early school years. They are his contributions to group activity.

Later School Years. It cannot be expected that all children will possess the same degree of talent in all areas of creative activity. It is probably true, however, that most children and young people

95

have the ability to exercise their imagination through one or another artistic medium if they receive sufficient encouragement to do so. Unfortunately, in the upper grades of the elementary school and especially in the high school, so much attention must be given to the mastery of factual material and the development of useful skills that the creative aspect of education is too much neglected.

Complete disregard for the so-called arts, or token attention to them, is to be regretted. Complete free expression, without guidance, in these areas of activity is equally undesirable. Whatever talent a young person possesses should be recognized by his teachers, and developed to the limit of his potentiality. This is a difficult task for a teacher who must "cover" a full curriculum of factual materials. Even so, there are beginnings on all school levels of attempts to help young people express in creative form their experiences, both in and outside the classroom.

DEVELOPMENT OF CREATIVE EXPRESSION

For the child as well as for the adult, creative expression in one form or another may satisfy one or both of two needs: (1) to serve as a release of pent-up emotions, (2) to re-organize existing knowledges or things in such a way that something new is developed which is more attractive or more useful than what has previously existed.

Bases of Expression. Whatever his purpose, the creator's activity is motivated by inner emotionalized urges. Free expression in one or another medium has been found to be a helpful form of therapy for the release of emotional conflict among the mentally disturbed. Sometimes the results are surprisingly good. So-called artistic production, however, is associated with the creative activity of the normal person who has more than average ability to reconstruct existing materials into new and probably better forms.

Creation implies mental exploration. The worth of the created product depends to some extent, at least, upon the scope of the creator's experience as well as upon his ability to understand all the details of the experience. Superior facility in the utilization of the medium of expression also is needed. The achievement of this facility is partly a matter of training but also may have its basis in inherent potentiality.

Progress in Development of Expression. The child's attempts to create are limited by his relatively meager background of

96

experience, even though he may possess some talent. Through the efforts of parents or teachers, the experiential background can be enriched and the urge to produce can be encouraged. For example, a class of first grade children were taken on a trip to view a bridge in a neighborhood that contained many tall apartment houses. The children were then encouraged to reproduce with paints on a large canvas what they saw. The results were interesting and varied. All were crude, but some gave evidence of a sensitivity to what they had seen — certain details of relative size and form were produced with remarkable accuracy for that age. Other children, who had not taken the trip, did little more than cover the paper with meaningless lines and blotches.

If an experience of this kind could be repeated from time to time with these children, it probably would be found that, with increasing maturity and experience, all the reproductions would improve and that some eventually would become commendable. The emotional satisfaction that accompanies a previously commended production would become a powerful motivating force toward improved techniques.

The creative experiences of the maturing child find their counterpart in creative efforts on the adult level. Continued enlargement of experience and refinement of techniques improved the creative efforts of the average person and result in superior production by the specially gifted.

Examples of progress in creative expression can be found in every field of production: art, music, literature, science, and mechanics. The automobile provides a striking illustration of gradual improvement in a product. It took scientific knowledge coupled with superior imaginative ability to give us the first horseless carriage. We may be amused when we view an automobile of the 1910 vintage. But as we compare the 1920 model with that which is common today and try to envisage what the automobile of the future may be like, we realize that creative activities are built upon existing production and are refined and improved as present knowledge is harnessed to superior creative ability.

It is imperative, therefore, to encourage children, from their earliest years onward, to engage in one or more creative activities. They should be motivated to express freely their creative interests and potentialities. They should be given opportunities to acquire background experience and to improve their techniques of production.

MEDIA FOR CREATIVE EXPRESSION

In any form of creative expression, an individual utilizes various phases of his total personality: mental, emotional, and motor. As he engages in creative activities, an integration of interests and processes is taking place that involves the whole person. If satisfaction in the activity, either on a lower or a higher level, is achieved, an awareness of self-realization is developed that is of great value to the child or the adult in his relationships with his associates.

The areas of creative expression are commonly classified as construction, drawing and painting, writing, music, and dancing. The development of these, more or less concurrently, from crude beginnings eventually may result in superior artistic creation. The developmental progress in these areas of creative expression is traced briefly in the following.

Early Manipulation. One of the child's earliest media of expression is the manipulation of blocks. He likes to handle them, and gradually to arrange them in one or another form, in terms of his level of maturation and his interest. Block-building follows a general pattern of developing skill.

The very young infant may do no more than touch a block, try to pick it up, or disregard it. Before he is one year old, however, he is likely to want to place blocks next to each other.

Rattles, dolls, small wagons, and miniature automobiles are included among the toys of most children. Toys such as these seem to have universal appeal to children. A child reaches for and manipulates his toy. He may bang it on the floor. He may try to pull it apart. He often attempts to combine his toys in one way or another; he may squeeze a small doll or other toy into his wagon, turn wheels with his fingers to make them go round, or even try to pull a toy apart to discover what is inside. By such activities, he is attempting to satisfy his curiosity. He is giving free rein to his growing imaginative powers. His behavior is not too different from that of the adult who is engaged in manipulatory activities, except that the adult usually has a specific purpose for his activity, although he may engage in the manipulation merely for the satisfaction that he achieves by so doing.

Painting, Design, and Art Crafts. The pictorial arts, design, and crafts are excellent media for the child to express his interests and emotionalized attitudes. He also receives training in attitudes of orderliness in the care of materials. He soon discovers that he needs to keep his materials in good condition and easily available, if he is to achieve the success that he desires from their utilization.

The younger child possesses an urge to express himself in clay modeling and painting with a large brush. He is not yet ready for the finer manipulatory movements. Hence, he should be encouraged to use the larger muscles as he works with easily handled materials and produces whole representations of objects with a minimum of detail.

In the kindergarten and the first grades of the elementary school, the children engage in finger painting, water painting, drawing with crayons, and craft activities. Each of these activities serves its particular function in helping the child develop his imaginative and emotional interests and possibilities.

Finger Painting. The combination of "colored mud," a table covered with oilcloth, a child standing at the table dressed in clothes that need not remain spotless, and the hands and arms bare to the elbows set the stage for a venture into finger painting. This means of self-expression, conceived by Ruth Shaw, has yielded good results with children through the second grade of the elementary school.

At first, the child places upon moistened paper about a teaspoonful of thick paint of a selected color. With the aid of both hands, he spreads the paint over the surface of the paper and then experiments freely with various designs. Sometimes, the arms as well as the fingers and hands are used. It may be possible for more mature children to work with more than one color.

Although the teacher may suggest and encourage, the resulting pattern is the child's. It is a form of play in which freedom of movement and unchecked imagination give him an opportunity to express himself without too much concern with the materials employed. An experienced and understanding adult can gain some insight into the child's emotional status as he watches the child at work and interpets the results. In fact, finger painting is said to have therapeutic value in dealing with children who suffer from one or another from of maladjustment.

Painting. In the nursery school and kindergarten, children first should be encouraged to paint with water on the blackboard with wide bristle brushes. The large sweeping movements thus made possible give good practice. The children are then introduced to easel painting using ready mixed paints, beginning with one color and gradually using red, blue, green, and violet. Later they may be allowed to include yellow and orange in their color selections. Third and fourth grade children can begin to experiment with the mixing of colors. By the time children reach the sixth grade they should have gained considerable facility with paints and brushes, and may work at their desks or tables on smaller paper and with smaller brushes.

The first attempts at painting may be very much like scribble drawing. As the child gains greater control of his muscles and enlarges his experiences, his painting includes greater detail. Some of the productions of a sixth grade may show considerable creative ability.

Drawing. The young child appears to gain a great deal of satisfaction from scribbing with a soft pencil or a crayon. He will cover many sheets of paper with all kinds of forms which are unrecognizable by the adult but which may be described proudly by the youngster as representing this or that common object in his immediate environment. After he has had some experience with water color, he can be allowed to experiment with colored crayons in the representation of shapes and designs.

Many sixth graders can produce commendable representations of particular subjects. Some become quite adept at illustrating stories, or representing objects or scenes which they have observed on a trip taken by the class to an interesting place. By this time, poster-designing, started in the nursery school or kindergarten, may be of such high quality that it can be exhibited in corridors or classrooms as notices of forthcoming events or as reminders of proper conduct. Either water colors or crayons are media that can be used for poster-designing.

Craft Activities. Children enjoy working with materials such as clay, blocks, yarn, wood, colored cloth, and puppets. They want to investigate and construct. Tactile experiences are most satisfying.

The young child likes to play with a lump of clay. He molds it into many apparently fantastic shapes. As he gains greater facility in the handling of this material, he can create interesting and, sometimes, worth-while objects. An increasing number of schools have glazing equipment so that each child can have at least one of his pieces fired.

Paper construction of objects is a fascinating method for a child to express his interests and feelings. As he measures, tears or cuts, folds, and fastens the paper and then decorates his product with paint or crayon, he is engaging in an activity that provides a wide range of expression of creative abilities and interests.

In representative art, children differ in their ability to achieve success. Whether the finished product can be said to be truly artistic is relatively unimportant. Every child should be provided with the opportunity to express himself through the craft media. At the same time, a child who displays talent should be encouraged to continue his efforts toward truly artistic production.

Creative Expression through Writing. Verbal creativity begins even before the child learns to write. Young children have a delightful manner of expressing themselves orally. They are direct and to the point. They formulate their own comparisons in making a point and stay within their limited experience. The sound and rhythm of words are grasped very early by some children. If their expressions are recorded, many rhymes or little poems can be found emerging from the lips of very young children. When it is given free rein, the imagination of children can produce ideas which are in the realm of fantasy, but which to the child are very real.

The Mechanics of Writing. When the child begins to express his ideas in written form he faces many difficulties. He must develop a vocabulary for expression, acquire the ability to form the characters needed in writing, and express his thoughts in acceptable patterns of grammatical usage and sentence structure. Unless he receives intelligent guidance during his early attempts at written expression, he gives so much attention to the mechanics of writing that free expression is inhibited. His writing then may become formal, stilted, and empty of any real expression of his thoughts and feelings.

The Child's Interests in Writing. The child has an urge to create. This is true of his written expression as well as of other forms of expression. Hence, insofar as he is able to do so, he at first should be encouraged to write down what he thinks with a minimum of attention given to the form in which it is said. Gradually, the child can be led to realize that if people are to understand what he is trying to tell them he must give some attention to the mechanics of written expression. To combine these two phases of writing is not easy. The adult who is guiding the child's learning must be ingenious in discovering ways to avoid sacrificing one for the other.

A child enjoys reporting an experience that he has had or writing a story that he has heard. As a result of the play of his imagination the actual experience may be much distorted as he reports it; important details of the story may be omitted and extraneous ideas added. Although the child's tendency to "embellish" can be disapproved of from the point of view of truthfulness of report, it is an indication of early groping toward creative expression and should not be discouraged entirely.

Development of Skill in Creative Writing. In order to help the child express his thoughts in acceptable form, a teacher sometimes dictates a short story or an account of an experience. The child then is encouraged to tell his own story or to report his own experience somewhat in the form of that which has been dictated. In this way the child gets the feel of good written expression.

The skill that the child gradually achieves in correct oral expression is likely to help him to improve his written expression. Also, such matters as punctuation and spelling need to be stressed. Once the child has developed interest in creating on paper, he usually is not too much inhibited in his creative writing by the fact that he must express himself correctly. A child who likes to read is likely to imitate the form of writing of his favorite authors, although at first he may attempt to use incorrectly words and expressions in these writings which happen to appeal to his imagination.

Eventually, each child can be expected to develop a characteristic style of composition, differing between the sexes. A boy tends to be more interested in topics of composition that are associated with his immediate experiences, especially sports and the like. He also tends to be careless in matters of spelling and punctuation, although his style is likely to be terse and to the point. A girl's writing tends to be more imaginative. Even an adolescent girl may go into flights of fancy. She also is more sensitive to the mechanics of writing, is a better speller, and gives more attention to proper punctuation and sentence structure.

Although the mechanics of writing are important, the creation of ideas is paramount. The second should never be sacrificed to the first. Many children can be taught to write correctly. Relatively few develop into the kind of adult who has a distinct and personal contribution to make to the field of literature. The cause of this situation may lie in the child's developmental potentialities, or the present inadequate methods of encouraging creative writing because of too great emphasis upon its mechanics, or sometimes a combination of both.

Rhythmic Expression. Although almost any form of activity possesses elements of rhythm, rhythmic expression usually is associated with music and the dance. Potential rhythmic sensitivity should be developed early in the child's life and refined through guided practice in vocal and instrumental music and through folk and social dancing.

Music. Most children are sensitive to musical rhythm. The young child responds to slumber songs. He enjoys hearing his mother sing simple little nursery rhymes, and may attempt to imitate the singing in his own inept fashion. Some babies appear to "sing" themselves to sleep, as they make inarticulate sounds that have a more or less recognizable rhythm.

The nursery school or kindergarten child enjoys participating in simple little songs as the teacher leads them and accompanies them on the piano, especially if the music has a quick tempo. During the elementary school years, children like to take part in group singing if the selections are not too difficult and if too much attention is not given to accuracy of production.

During the middle years, some boys and girls take great delight in singing around the home. They are giving expression to their feelings. They tend to improvise, not only in rhythm but also in words.

Children differ in their ability to carry a tune. Some are much more sensitive to correct pitch, time, timbre, or tone quality than are others. Whether this is an inherent lack or the result of inadequate training is a matter of opinion. Psychologists who have given considerable attention to the development of musical ability, such as Seashore, believe that musical ability is not a general capacity, but that individuals may differ in their possession of one or more aspects of musical expression.

As in other areas of creative activity, a child should be allowed considerable freedom of expression of his feelings and emotions. At the same time he needs training in correct expression. There is a difference of opinion among school personnel on both the elementary and secondary school levels concerning the relative merits of allowing children to sing popular songs during school assembly periods, for example, and of spending much time during assembly and classroom periods in training young people to produce correctly appropriate and more or less classical selections.

There probably is need for some free singing as well as for training in mastering relatively difficult music. Some children can be encouraged to create attractive little melodies for which words can be written by classmates. Some very good class songs have been composed by children.

Many of the suggestions concerning vocal music presented in the foregoing are applicable to creative expression through instrumental music. Young children seem to have an urge to make noises. The young child may like to bang his mother's pots and pans. Weird sounds may result from his experimentation with pot covers. He derives a great deal of pleasure from shaking his rattle, or bells that may be attached to his toys.

Later, a boy, especially, enjoys tooting a horn. Playing a harmonica also is a source of pleasure to a boy and, sometimes, a girl.

Systematic training in the playing of an instrument probably should follow the gaining of some skill in vocal music. Traditionally, the piano is the accepted instrument for beginnings in this form of musical expression. Children seem to respond more willingly, however, to training in the mastery of percussion instruments. Even as early as the first years of the elementary school may be a propitious time to give children some experience with the simpler wind instruments.

Although the ability to perform adequately is a social assist during adolescent and adult years, it is not wise to force a child to "study" instrumental music. Unless the child or adolescent wants to do so, the time devoted to the weekly lesson and the daily practice period becomes irksome. School bands and orchestras provide much better media for the average child to give expression to his interest in music. Association with his peers and the thrill of performing for special school events, such as sport contests and the school assembly, are most satisfying to the young person. Many schools have set up beginners' and advanced bands and orchestras in which even young people with mediocre ability have been stimulated to achieve acceptable performance.

The Dance. As soon as a child has gained adequate control of his gross body muscles he delights in running, skipping, hopping, and jumping. Even the one-year-old may move his entire body to music. The child of nursery school and kindergarten age experiences great satisfaction from clapping his hands or marching to the accompaniment of stirring music. At this stage, he may not keep time accurately with the music.

During the early school years, children begin to participate in group games that may include simple dance steps. *Musical Chairs* and *Follow the Leader* afford opportunities for experiencing body rhythm, and include beginnings of dance steps. Later, greater control of body and feet movement and increased sensitivity to rhythm are acquired as children learn to participate in folk dances, which become increasingly complex through the high school years.

The ability to participate in social dancing is an important phase of the growing-up process. Girls become interested in this form of expression sooner than do most boys. The custom, prevalent among some parents, of sending their elementary-school-aged children to dancing school for training in social dancing usually is enjoyed by little girls but constitutes an embarrassing chore for many boys. Even on the secondary level, many boys seem to be self-conscious, especially when they are expected to dance with girls of their own age group. One reason for this attitude may be found in the fact that girls mature physically earlier than boys.

The boy or girl who shows unusual sensitivity to the rhythm of the dance should be provided opportunities for special training as early as seems desirable. The dance is an excellent medium for creativity, in the improvisation of original steps or dance sequences. The young child should not be expected to devote so much time and energy to his dance practice, however, that all-round healthy development is interfered with, or that he thereby is deprived of participation in other interesting and worth-while activities suitable to his age.

Appreciation of the Arts. Relatively few young people will become superior performers in any one or more of the expression arts. Many more than now is the case could be encouraged to give self-satisfying expression to their interests and feelings in at least one of the creative media.

Most normal young people can be stimulated toward an appreciation of artistic masterpieces. Both elementary and secondary schools attempt to provide opportunities for the development of appreciations. Too often, however, the materials presented and the methods of presenting them appeal to the intellect rather than to the imagination and emotions. Sometimes children are expected to appreciate beauty of expression that is too complex or advanced for their level of maturation. Undue concern with the general life pattern of the creator of the masterpiece or with the details of the production may nullify any desirable ends to be achieved. Artistic appreciation is an individual experience. The amount or kind of appreciation that has resulted from a "lesson" in appreciation cannot be tested in the same way as is possible for testing mastery of factual material. Properly presented, artistic masterpieces can arouse in the young person sensitivities and emotional reactions that serve him well as tension-releasers and stimulators of his own imagination and creative facilities.

CHILDREN'S PLAY

Play or recreational activity of one kind or another satisfies an individual's urge for freedom of action. From infancy to adulthood, he is impelled to engage in various forms of more or less spontaneous "play" activity.

Meaning of Play. Play or recreational activity can be defined as the activity in which a person engages when he is free to do what he wants to do. A child does not have to learn to *want* to play or to do any one of the many things from which he derives pleasure for so much of his time.

Relation to Other Forms of Activity. Attempts have been made to differentiate among play, work, and drudgery. In play, the satisfaction is found in the activity itself; work is activity aimed at the achievement of a future goal; drudgery is an activity engaged in because of an outer impelling force, with little or no personal interest in the activity itself or in its supposed end or goal. There is too much overlapping in these specific interpretations to make the distinctions among them of practical value.

Work that is pleasurable and creative takes on the aspects of play. Temporarily, at least, the participant in the work activity is unmindful of the goal toward which he supposedly is striving. He is "working" for the sheer joy that he derives from the activity. Contrariwise, a presumably play activity may constitute a problem situation, even though there seems to be no eventual goal to be achieved. The individual works at the play activity with such seriousness and intensity that tensions and feelings of frustration may be induced. So-called forms of play, such as competitive sports, may be work in a real sense, if the main objective is to win championship status. Also, an activity that begins as drudgery may arouse so much interest in the person after he has started it that he derives pleasure from it.

Characteristics of Play. Fundamentally, play is any activity that is all-absorbing, gives pleasure, represents some degree of creativeness, and is not concerned with the attainment of an end result, apart from the activity itself. During childhood, play is more informal than it is later. With increase in age, play activities decrease in number, but there is an increase in the specific time devoted to a particular kind of play activity.

Many benefits accrue to the child and adult from play activity. Participation in play or recreational activity is affected by many factors that direct the form it may take.

Theories of Play. The fact that the desire to play appears to be a natural urge has intrigued philosophers and psychologists since earliest time. Various theories have been presented in explanation of this aspect of child activity.

Play as Release of Surplus Energy. This theory, sometimes referred to as the Schiller-Spencer theory, is perhaps one of the oldest. Observations of a child's apparently aimless activity led to the conclusion that through his continuous play he is exercising his boundless energies. This theory cannot be accepted in its entirety, however. A child may seem to expend a great deal of energy in his constant laughing, manipulating, running, and jumping. Yet, some play of children is quiet and can be engaged in even though the child is ill.

Play as Recapitulation. The theory of play as the recapitulation of racial experiences was propounded by Hall. From his observation of children's play he concluded that a child unconsciously relives the various stages of civilization, beginning with the primitive stage. By the time the child is about nine years old, according to Hall, the "big Injun" period has been reached as evidenced by interest in pottery, bows and arrows, and other things and activities associated with Indian life and creative skill.

This theory once influenced school programs for the middle elementary years, but has lost its appeal. It is no longer believed that children inherit acquired traits and characteristics. Moreover, their play interests do not appear to follow any such regular pattern.

Play as Preparation for Future Activity. According to Groos, a Swiss psychologist, play is a form of inherent drive toward preparation for common adult patterns of life. The little girl's playing with her dolls is preparing her for motherhood. A boy's mechanical manipulation represents unconscious drives toward the development of mechanical skill needed in adult life.

Modern psychologists agree that the child engages in play activity in response to inner urges. His play activities, however, are neither conscious nor unconscious attempts to prepare himself for adulthood. He may learn much through his play that will be of value to him later, but the gaining of knowledge or skill is a by-product rather than the fundamental purpose of play.

Play as a Life Activity. At present, the most generally accepted theory of play is the one propounded by John Dewey. He believed that activity is the essence of organismic life. Individual activity may be expressed in many forms. The young child's chief business of life is play. As he grows older, he participates in various forms of activites that either may be directed toward the attainment of a goal, as in purposeful work, or may be characterized by the spirit of free, non-goal direction, or play.

Varieties of Play. Play is spontaneous and imaginative. To the adult it may seem to be aimless, but to the child it may be constructive. The play activities of the young child are simple. As the child matures, his play activities usually become more complex and elaborate.

The very young child plays alone. He gradually passes through the stage of playing alongside of other children of either sex, and finally derives great satisfaction from playing with peer groups, usually of the same sex. The play or recreational activities of the adolescent become increasingly selective and individualistic, and may be engaged in either with groups of the same sex or with mixed groups.

Play activities are somewhat related to mental and health status. The bright child tends to be very much interested in reading, creative activities, guessing games, card games, and games of chance. He usually is only mildly interested in social play activities, exept in groups that represent his own intellectual level. The mentally retarded child usually avoids competition in intellectual games but may develop considerable skill in a more vigorous play activity.

A delicate child is forced to limit his play activities to reading, creative activities, and quiet games. These are solitary or shared with a small group of children. The healthy, energetic young person usually spends every minute of his free time in one or another variety of his many play interests.

A child's play interests and activities are influenced by the customs of his culture in much the same way as his other developing patterns of behavior are affected by existing traditions. Younger children observe and eventually imitate the games of older children, just as the latter were introduced to their forms of play by still older children.

Various forms of culture continue their accustomed activities. As the different geographical areas of the world are being brought together through improved intercommunication, however, there seems to be both a leveling and an expansion of play interests. For example, little Japanese boys are becoming interested in "Wild West" stories and engage in cowboy activities, dressed in costumes that have been sent to them by American friends.

Children reared in rural areas engage in generally vigorous out-of-door activities, but may not have many opportunities for out-of-school social play. They usually have relatively few opportunities to attend motion picture theaters and similar places of amusement.

City and town children may be restricted in their out-of-door play to adult-supervised playgrounds that have available play equipment. Urban children also have opportunities for attendance at various centers of amusement and entertainment. There are advantages in either kind of environment, however, that should be made available for all children.

A poor environment may afford fewer play opportunities, both in the home and out, than do the more favorable environmental areas. There usually are more children in the poor neighborhoods, so that playmates are available. These children often are left to their own resources to find places and materials with which to play. The generally poor health of children in slum areas may militate against their interest in constructive play activities. Furthermore, the older children of large families or children of working mothers may need to devote their out-of-school time to the performance of home chores rather than to play activity.

Climatic conditions also affect the kind of play in which children are likely to engage. The play activities of children living in warm countries are relatively sedentary, whereas children living in colder climates usually excel in vigorous games and sports. Definite seasonal changes to be found in some geographic areas are reflected in differences of play activities.

Importance of Play. Free activity that may seem to be relatively purposeless affects every area of a child's personality: physical, mental, emotional, and social.

As the child manipulates, vocalizes, walks, runs, skips, and jumps, he is strengthening his muscles and improving motor co-ordination. At the same time, he learns much about the world around him as he explores, collects, reads, attends concerts and plays, visits museums, and views appropriate motion picture and television programs.

Children gain much pleasure from imaginative play, such as make-believe or dramatics. Original rhymes or little poems, drawings, and dance steps are examples of creative activities that are emotionally satisfying.

A normal child wants and seeks peer companionship. He learns the art of give-and-take as he participates in many forms of group play. He acquires an appreciation of the value to himself as well as to others of co-operation, honesty, and good sportsmanship.

The value of play as a tension-releaser is evidenced in the utilization of play therapy in the treatment of emotionally disturbed children. As a child, uninhibited by adult control, engages in free play, he thereby is given an opportunity to release any fears, resentments, or frustration resulting from too rigid control of his behavior or from unfavorable environmental conditions. Recreational therapy serves a similar purpose for patients in hospitals for the mentally ill.

Adjustment through Play. Throughout his life span an individual needs to experience a balanced program of work and play. However, all activity should not be reduced to the play level. School activities need to be motivated to interest the child and to help him recognize their value. At the same time he should be helped to develop an attitude toward work as activity directed toward the achievement of a goal and an attitude of purposeful pride in the completion of a task. Motivated activities rather than mere play is desired.

The child needs change of activity. He needs release from the strain of purposeful activity, no matter how satisfying the activity may be. He needs to participate in those forms of activities in which his interest lies in the activity itself and in the physical and mental relaxation that can result. The child needs to learn healthful procedures in his play. He needs to learn attitudes of cooperation as well as of good sportsmanship.

It is essential that adequate provision be made in the school for free play and organized games as a relief from the more serious activities. These recreational periods should not be so short that they afford insufficient relaxation, nor so long that the child tires or loses interest in his school work.

The child never should be punished for failure in his studies by denying him to participate in play activities, since this may engender an attitude of dislike and resentment of his required duties. An understanding of both work and play should be developed in the child by the school personnel. He needs to understand that each can provide for him desirable satisfactions and values.

As a means of furthering a child's physical, emotional and social development, parents and teachers should provide for him interesting and health-giving recreational activities. These need to be attention-gaining and not tension-arousing. The young child's activity in the home and in the nursery school and kindergarten is play-oriented.

The growing power of sensation and perception of the child, the refinement of his body control and speech habits, the increase of his mental ability, his growing recognition of his emotional states, and his developing appreciation of his social world are helpful to him in his early adjustment to his social environment. Parents and teachers need to be aware of his rate and kind of physical development so that they can adjust the environment to his developing needs and abilities.

Older children are gregarious and seek companionship. They yearn for and need to be exposed to an enlarging social experience as they engage in activities with other boys and girls of their own age. They desire opportunities for self-expression in group situations. They enjoy competition with their peers and are eager to win the approval and admiration of them. The gang spirit is strong during this period and can be utilized for the formation of educationally valuable club projects. Through these they can develop maturity of judgement and social ease. They also can discover that the rights of others are to be respected if they wish to gain and keep friends.

CHAPTER 9

The Dynamics of Children's Behavior

A child's attitudes, his immediate and more permanent interests, and the factors within and outside himself that are likely to influence his behavior exercise a significant effect upon his life pattern at any stage of his development. The individual's degree of successful development as a child and his accomplishments as an adult depend in great measure upon the direction taken by these aspects during the growing-up period. Attitudes and interests will determine the degree of success in learning that an individual child may expect to achieve at any time in his development.

Interest and motive are basic to a child's activities. The child is not born with his attitudes or his particular interests. They develop out of his innate potentialities as he is motived to attend to various phases of his inner and outer world and to engage in many different kinds of activities. Satisfactory attitudes and interests must be aroused and developed if he is to be stimulated toward the full development of his capabilities.

DEVELOPMENT OF ATTITUDES

Attitudes are not static. Certain generally displayed attitudes of a child or of an adult are considered to be habitual for him. Yet attitudes can be changed as newer experiences make formerly exhibited attitudes untenable.

Meaning of Attitude. An attitude is a readiness, inclination, or tendency to act toward inner or external elements in accordance with the individual's acquaintance with them. An attitude grows out of an individual's understanding and appreciation of a situation and his emotional response to it. Inner stimuli are involved. The extent to which these inner stimuli encourage or

112

inhibit behavior in a particular situation may be considered one's attitude toward the situation.

A person may be unaware of the attitude that causes him to respond as he does toward a person or object, or in a particular situation. When attitudes seem to be relatively inactive, they may be considered one's attitude toward the situation.

A person may be unaware of the attitude that causes him to respond as he does toward a person or object, or in a particular situation. When attitudes seem to be relatively inactive, they may be considered to be elements that compose one's *disposition*. When attitudes give evidence of strong feeling tones, they may be called *sentiments*.

In his day-by-day activities, a child or an adult constantly is influenced by the behavior or expressed opinions of other people. The home, the school, the place of work, the social group with which he is associated, and the various media of communication (newspapers, magazines, books, radio, television, motion pictures, and the like) exert a tremendous impact upon the individual's thoughts, feelings, and interests. Hence, consciously or unconsciously he acquires attitude patterns that may change from time to time when his own interests as well as environmental influences change. Attitudes that are common for a culture are likely to exercise a potent effect upon individuals who are reared in the culture. One member of a group may become so forceful an exponent of his attitudes that other members of the group, temporarily or more permanently, seem to be completely swayed by the expressed attitudes of their leader.

Formation of Attitudes. Attitudes are acquired through experience. An individual learns to like baseball, badminton, oranges, or Buick cars. Similarly, he learns to dislike unkempt clothes, dirty faces, or rude or dishonest persons. The bases of a person's likes and dislikes result from the degree of satisfaction or annoyance that he has associated with the objects, persons, or situations toward which, for one reason or another, he has developed a favorable or unfavorable attitude. The developed attitude then is reflected in the individual's overt behavior.

The Power of Suggestion. Imitation and suggestion are potent molders of attitudes, especially during childhood years. The child is sensitive to the expressed attitudes of his parents, teachers, and playmates. Sometimes unconsciously, he reflects the likes and dislikes of his associates. He does not know the reason for his attitude, but it appears to be the desirable one for him to have. The power of imitation can be examplified by a young person's imitated attitudes toward one or another religious belief, political affiliation, or national or racial background.

Suggestion exerts a great influence upon the direction and development of attitudes. This suggestion can be given by word or by gesture. Attitudes alter the developmental patterns, as the child continues to experience a give-and-take relationship between himself and his parents, his teachers, his peer associates, and other environmental stimuli. The effect upon a child's attitude of adult suggestion may vary with the situation and the child's interest at the moment. If the young person is highly emotionalized or generally resentful of adult behavior toward him, suggestion may influence his attitude but in a direction opposite to that which was intended.

Persistence of Attitudes. To the extent that the feeling tone that accompanies one or another of a person's experiences tends to be satisfying or annoying, his attitude toward that experience continues to persist and can be said to become habitual. For example, during the preadolescent or early adolescent stage of development a young person may be allergic to a particular kind of food, such as strawberries. The eating of the strawberries may cause facial blemishes to appear. This is extremely annoying to the self-conscious young person and he develops an unfavorable attitude toward the berries. This attitude may persist long after the actual allergy disappears.

Progressive Development of Attitudes. Simple feelings of well-being and physical discomfort are more characteristic of infants and very young babies than is any organized pattern of attitude. During the first year of life, the well-cared-for baby usually exhibits what might be termed affectionate responses to those adults who form the human factors of his environment but is shy with strangers.

During the next two or three years, the normal child begins to develop more definite attitudes of possessiveness and desire for approval. He may resent attention given to other children, and develop an attitude of resistance to the suggestions or wishes of others.

As the child advances through the elementary school years he acquires more or less definite attitudes toward himself and his peer

114

and older associates. He becomes more independent. His likes and dislikes, based upon previous and present experiences, are more readily recognized by himself. He continues to respond to approval and disapproval, but his attitudes in this respect are more reasonable and better related to specific situations and conditions. By the time the young person enters adolescent years, he probably has acquired many attitude patterns that may be desirable or undesirable and that have been developing gradually from early childhood onward.

Significance of Attitudes. People come to evaluate a child's personality in terms of his expressed attitudes, especially those that show themselves in situations that include other persons. Adults and other children approve of the young person who is generally friendly, agreeable, and co-operative. Social disapproval is given to irritable, unfriendly, or extremely selfish attitudes or behavior.

Too often a child's motives or the reasons for his attitudes, especially those that are unfavorable, are not understood by parents, teachers, or other adults who are associated with the child. They may condemn when they should understand the situation that gave rise to the child's attitude and attempt to improve it.

Since a child's social status is determined large by his attitude toward others, concern for the welfare of his associates is an attitude which he should be encouraged to adopt at an early age. A child can develop a readiness to conform or not to conform. This *set in attitude* stimulates some actions and inhibits others. Certain set attitudes habitually motivate the behavior of the young child in the home, the older child in the school, and the adolescent in the presence of members of the other sex. A person who has learned to forget self and to be of service to his associates has developed some of the characteristics essential to the gaining of appreciation from others.

DEVELOPMENT OF INTERESTS

It is sometimes difficult to distinguish between an attitude and an interest, since a close relationship exists between the two. An attitude can be regarded as relatively deep-rooted, general, and continuous. An interest, however, may be more fleeting and inconsistent. A persistent interest may take on some of the general characteristics of an attitude.

Meaning of Interest. The reason given for an individual's

115

engaging in one or another form of activity is commonly that of "interest." Interest may be the affective experience aroused by the activity itself or it may be the motivating force that directs attention to a person, an object, or an activity.

If a child's curiosity has been aroused sufficiently for him to want to spend energy in the solution of a problem or in the search for further information concerning a favorite motion picture star or a scientist, he is exhibiting interest in the activity. If an experiment is started in a science class and the child must leave before it has been finished but does not want to go until he has completed it, there is evidence of interest in the activity.

Children acquire their interests as they live in their environment. They have few if any natural interests. Interests are closely associated with motives, drives, and the emotional responses and attitudes that are developing. A child's early interests are a part of his dynamic pattern of growing capacities. His interests, attitudes, and abilities usually keep pace through the early years of his development. It is difficult to teach a child to walk before he shows an interest in learning to walk. This interest must wait for maturation. The same principle holds for any mental or motor activity. Unless interest in the activity is manifested by the learner he is not likely to be successful in his learning.

Interest and Activity. Interest can both be the cause of and result from experience. Interest aroused as the result of an activity can become a stimulus to participation again in the same or a similar activity.

Choice of Interests. The activities chosen by children vary widely. One young child may prefer to play in a sand pile, or with dolls or crayons. Another child may spend much time riding a tricycle, playing favorite records, listening to the radio, or watching television. Still others follow the lead of a particular child or children with whom they happen to be associating at the time.

The leader can do much to stimulate interest among children. For best behavior development, however, children should be permitted to utilize whatever materials are available for the expression of their interests and then be given freedom of activity in expressing them so long as behavior conforms to desirable social standards. The example set by adults can give direction to the kind of activities that are selected by the children.

Relation of Interests to Activity. A child's interests do not grow

116

as separate entities. They are learned and developed in relation to his other behavioral aspects. Adults, therefore, should aim to help the child to cultivate those interests that will be most rewarding to him rather than be guided by the interests that the child may happen to display at the moment.

Early success in an activity may so stimulate interest that the child will wish to spend much time at it and thus develop some degree of skill in it. Lack of successful first efforts may so discourage an otherwise able child that he will hesitate to continue or return to the activity. He thus is denied normal development in it. Some of the child's tendencies to be afraid or overcautious in a social situation can be traced to unsatisfying earlier experiences. With a rise in competence usually goes a corresponding rise in interest. If external pressures are applied for increase in skill at the expense of the child's ability, his interest may decrease.

Reading Interests. Children enjoy hearing stories read to them long before they are able to understand the words of the story. The reader's facial expression, the rhythmic flow of words, and the sound of the reader's voice appear to stimulate the child. The young child begins to show interest in reading through such other activities as manipulating books, magazines, and pictures, and looking at pictures and emotionalizing as he identifies them.

Reading interests of children vary with age. The comic book is a source of great interest for many years. Children enjoy having comic books read to them even before they can do more than look at the pictures. Many children of three and four show keen interest in these books. At the same time animal stories, fanciful stories, and stories of other little boys and girls fascinate them to the point that they will sit and listen to them for a long period at a time.

Children show an interest in literature that is either fiction or fact. During this elementary school years they thrill at stories dealing with the impossible but are just as eager to read stories of real situations that deal with travel, sports, biography, geography, and science. The reading interests of the average adolescent boy differs from that of the adolescent girl. A boy is likely to be interested in reading material about travel, sports, adventure, mechanics, science, and the lives of famous men. Although a girl may give evidence of some interest in books usually favored by boys, she is more likely to read romantic novels, stories about girls, and poetry. The reading habits of adolescent boys and girls are beginning to show greater similarity than formerly was the case. Librarians exert a great influence on book choices of young readers.

Radio and Television Interests. The average child of school age spends hours in listening to radio broadcasts or viewing and listening to television programs. Estimates on time spent in such activity by the average child run as high as from two to four hours daily. The kind of program in which the child is interested varies with the age and the sex of the child. Programs of the type that dramatize fairy stories and other make-believe adventures or those that involve chitchat decline in popularity as the child grows older. The child may be conditioned by the programs selected by adults. He sometimes continues to enjoy adult-selected programs because, through experience, his interests have been developed along such lines.

Sport programs of all kinds hold the interest of boys and are gaining in their interest value for girls. Programs that feature news and current events are among those that are listened to with interest by older boys and girls. In general, boys prefer programs involving crime and violence. Girls show a higher preference for programs involving domestic drama or featuring their favorite movie stars. Girls also like programs in which a child character plays an important role or in which love scenes dominate.

Interest in the use of radio and television programs is so keen that school officials have been introducing them in increasing number into the regular school program. The child has the interest. It is a challenge to curriculum-makers to provide the kind of stimuli through radio and television that will be of most benefit to the developing child.

Motion Picture Interests. Motion pictures are observed on the average of about once in every two weeks by children between the ages of five and eight. About 20 per cent of the children in this age range probably attend the "movies" two or more times per week. Comedy is of greatest interest to them. Boys show a greater interest than do girls in movies that include mystery, westerns, gangster themes, and news. Girls prefer educational films or love stories.

As with radio and television programs, many of the films are produced for adults and therefore are not suited to children. This criticism holds also for some of the films that are now being shown on television, as well as some of the television vaudeville programs.

118

Interest in Comics. Comics are read by individuals of all levels of reading age, an estimated total of more than 60,000,000 presons. The largest percentage of readers falls between the ages of eight and fifteen years. The daily paper is not felt to be complete unless it includes one or more comic strips.

Many comic strips are thought-provoking and have educational value, but too many comic books are printed on poor-grade paper and in such small type that injury to the eyes is likely to result from reading them. Since producers of these comic books have employed trained educators to assist in the construction of the stories, their content has shown some improvement.

The comic books that can be bought on most newsstands are written to appeal to a wide variety of tastes. "Mickey Mouse" appeals to young children and "Superman" to older children, especially boys. Comic strips and comic books are read partly because they are funny and partly because they portray a story in picture form, with little reading matter necessary to complete the idea. The interest value of comics and the ideas embodied in them are sufficient to warrant the salvaging of these values for children's literature by upgrading them in form and content.

Interest in Play. Play arises spontaneously from an inner urge. A child need not be taught to play. He engages early in activities that are performed for the sheer joy of the doing. In his daily activities he moves freely through the motor responses of adaptive behavior. He utilizes his language and personal and social behavior as he expands in his social relationships, beginning with his mother. He is active during his waking hours. For him this activity is play.

Play interest never ceases to be a dominant influence in the child's life. This interest shows gradations during his growing-up period. The eighteen-month-old child wants to play in sand and mud; by two years of age he mixes stones with the sand, but by five years he does not like to be restricted to the sand box. Later, in school, the sand box becomes an excellent outlet for his imaginative play.

A child may tend to play excessively with a particular toy. This obsessive interest is more common among boys than among girls. The boy also may be engrossed with one activity at one time and another at another time. He may start to play with his trains and then become interested in climbing. By the age of about seven he seems to show a succession of intensified interests.

119

Effect of Many Interests. Children and young people are faced with conflicting interests. It is sometimes difficult for them to understand that immediate interests may have to be sacrificed in order that more lasting and perhaps more worth-while ones may be satisfied. A child is faced with a choice between using his ten cents to buy an ice cream cone now or waiting until later when he can use that ten cents to satisfy a more important need.

A child needs rest and sleep, but his interest in his play activities sometimes is so great that he rebels at having to stop them. The struggle to induce a child to go to bed on time is too common in some homes. The situation may become series if he has to be almost forced to go to bed and is in so excited a state that he cannot fall asleep. This offers a different kind of confict from those in which the child is given a choice of either of two interests to follow at a given time.

One interest may command his attention to the exclusion of other equally desirable and worth-while interests. Interest in people, interest in things, and interest in oneself are equally important. A child must learn to strike a balance in his interests so that he may satisfy all of them. He also must learn that immediate interest may have to give way to the fulfillment of a more remote goal.

Vocational efficiency is built upon the ability of an individual to decide early upon his major vocational interest. The developing individual may become intrigued with the many expanding interests he discovers. In this way, conflict may arise concerning the one of his various interests he should decide upon. Likewise, the numerous extracurricular activities provided in some schools stimulate some young people to want to participate in most, if not all, of them. A growing young person's time and energy are limited. He needs help in discovering where his major interests lie so that he may concentrate on them.

Within the limits of a child's ability, energy, and time, multiple interests are to be encouraged. When the child reaches adulthood he will need to develop interests outside his regular work. The beginnings of such leisure-time activities or hobbies should be encouraged during the child's school life. Although the growing individual needs guidance in the matter of narrowing interests down to workable limits, he should have freedom of selection of those in which he will engage.

Effect of Interest on Work. The completion of any activity requires effort. Even the young child should learn that things do not do themselves. The more strenuous or difficult the work, the more effort is required to complete it. If the child has sufficient interest in his home chores or school tasks, the activity is reduced for him to the play level. He needs to realize, however, that although the task is interesting it still is work aimed at the achievement of a goal.

The younger as well as the older child may spend a relatively long time in attempts to find the solution to a problem in which he is interested but will give up a much simpler problem because of his lack of interest in it. Interest based upon his ability to perform will spur him on toward productive efforts and usually will bring him success within the limits of his ability.

Interest and Fatigue. Fatigue is produced by excessive physical activity. During physical activity poisons or toxins accumulate within the body and affect the muscles. Actual fatigue rarely results from mental activity except when it is accompanied by physical overwork. In most cases, the so-called fatigue represents loss of interest in the activity in which the individual is engaged.

A child may report that his eyes hurt as the result of extended study. The same child then may experience no feelings of fatigue if he picks up an interesting story and continues his reading. A change of activity usually serves as a release of fatigue factors that may have been operating under definite concentration on a problem.

It is unusual for a young person to become so interested in his school work that he studies beyond the limits of healthful endurance. He may sit in one position so long, however, that it is injurious to his health to sit longer without change in position. If he becomes very much interested in what he is doing he may work long past his regular meal or bed time. This kind of behavior may produce genuine fatigue. The child should plan his daily work and study schedule so as to avoid such situations.

Children need rest and relaxation. Rest periods should be frequent for young children but need not be long in duration. the young school child should be given opportunities for frequent change in activities. As he grows older the length of the work or study period can be increased.

MOTIVATION OF BEHAVIOR

Human drives and urges serve as inner motivations of behavior.

These organic and psychological drives include those connected with bodily needs, such as hunger, thirst, sleep, and sex, or other needs that sometimes are not completely recognized by associates. Some of these other drives are the urge to be with other people, to collect, to be curious, to seek attention from others or to be recognized and approved by them, to succeed, to be superior, to be secure, and to experience adventure.

Sources of Motivation. A child's motives usually reflect the influence of parents or friends upon his inner drives. The blocking of these motives produces emotional states associated with frustration. Such frustrations may be experienced in one way or another by the individual from early childhood through adulthood.

Although human beings, like other animals, respond to organic drives, the desire to conform to socially acceptable modes of behavior is one of the most potent of human motives. The very young child is interested primarily in satisfying organic needs. He never loses these organic drives. As he matures, social stimuli awaken urges that modify the ways in which the biological drives are satisfied.

The behavior of children is conditioned for good social living as this principle is utilized in the home and in the school. The strong urges that the child has toward satisfying his personal needs and cravings are conditioned early by training. In other words, he learns to change his goals to correspond with acceptable behavior as he attempts to satisfy his appetites, ambitions, cravings, and interests.

Meaning and Characteristics of Motivation. Motivation is an activating force that affects every area of human behavior. It influences a simple act, the motive of which is obvious, as well as a more complex, formal activity pattern. It is complex in its functioning even in those activities associated with the satisfaction of body requirements of food, water and oxygen. Motivation pertains to drive, incentive and homeostasies. It is believed to be a combination of forces that initiate, give direction to, and continue behavior toward a goal.

Human drive pertains to a condition of the child in which his behavior is activated or directed toward a specific goal. An incentive or goal pertains to that which affects the child in such a way as to cause a reduction of the drive or its elimination. For example, food is an incentive to satisfy the hunger drive. Money is an incentive to encourage a child to perform a task.

Homeostasis is a term used to describe the equilibrium-preserving function that takes place within the individual. This is a physiological equilibrium that is kept in balance through the functioning of various biological drives. Once a child's physiological equilibrium has been disturbed, the behavior that is activated ceases only when the goal is attained and the equilibrium has been restored. A food imbalance for example, needs to be corrected in order for the child to reduce or lose his drive for food. Proper intake of food will complete the process of homeostasis.

Motivated behavior is activated behavior. Except for his hours of sleep and his other periods of quiescent behavior, the child is an active being. Motivation represents the difference between being asleep or awake, relaxed or tense. In motivated behavior the child is in a state of readiness to become active or to continue his activity. Thus is set up a motivational sequence that causes the reduction or elimination or the drive. A thirst drive, for example, activates the incentive that affects the intensity of the drive that eventually reduces or eliminates it.

Motivated behavior tends to persist, to be energized and to display itself in a number of ways. It has continuity. The child will tend to pursue the goal in terms of the strength of the desire. Usually an increase in hunger is accompanied by an increase of food-seeking behavior; an increase in interest to become a member of the team is accompanied by an increase cooperation in practice. The strength of the motive is closely associated with the strength of the effort.

Motivated behavior may take the form of exploratory variation if the child fails to attain a desired goal. For example, during a child's first day in a new school he may exhibit variations in behavior in order to earn acceptance. He may display his possessions, or attempt to prove his mental or physical ability. If either fails he turns to another and another until he gains acceptance. The teacher can lessen the child's need to engage in acceptance-seeking activities by taking the initiative and introducing the new pupil to the members of the class.

Proper emotional tonus gives power to human motives and drives. Strongly motivated situations encourage emotional energization. When the motive is strong but there is delay or resistance, the child's behavior shows increased energy through emotional tension. The displayed behavior may take the form of anger, anxiety, fear, aggression or other emotional expression.

IMPORTANCE OF MOTIVES,
INCENTIVES AND COMPETITION

Motives. A motive stimulates an individual to activity which goes beyond the achievement of immediate satisfaction in goal-seeking. His behavior is influenced by the amount of satisfaction or annoyance that he experiences in any situation in which his urges and interests are involved. Motives in any situation in which his urges and interests are involved. Motives act like dynamic forces. They arise out of natural urges or acquired interests and affect an individual's thoughts, emotions, and behavior. By means of praise or some other form of extrinsic reward, a child may be stimulated to do more and perhaps better work. For the child the motive is that of recognition rather than the mastery of information or the completion of a task.

It is not always a simple matter to discover the actual stimulus which motivates a child's behavior. Although in early childhood his behavior drives are relatively simple, these increase in number and complexity as he matures. To the older child, praise becomes a more potent motivating force than an extrinsic award. The extrinsic award still may be important, but the child becomes more selective in the matter of the kind of award to which he responds.

Motives serve to energize, select, and direct the activities of children. The whole pattern of inner compulsion is so interwoven that it is impossible to identify separately any one function of motives. The chief role of parents and teachers in this connection is to aid in giving the child those mental and emotional sets that will cause him to want to learn what he should or to behave as he should. The success of his learning and adjustment will determine the achievement of the goals in which he has been helped to become interested.

Value of Incentives. An incentive can be considered to be any force or stimulus that will impel a child to do something which in its absence he would not be interested in doing. The child who is learning to walk is provided an incentive or a near goal of a chair or a person. An incentive must be within a child's reach, both in space and time, and must be within his understanding. He must feel that it is worth while and that it can be achieved.

Incentive to learning will not be completely effective until sufficient maturation has taken place. For example, the child who is delayed in the development of reading readiness is not likely to be stimulated toward productive reading by even the best incentives that can be presented. Extrinsic incentives can play a good role in motivating a child. Nevertheless, the reward should be incidental to the real goal. Incentives that are continuous in their effect, therefore, should be utilized so that they help the child hold his interest over a relatively long period of time. For example, a boy who is a retarded reader is very much interested in mechanics but is not able to comprehend the printed directions for constructing a model airplane. The interest will act as an incentive toward improvement, under guidance, in his reading comprehension.

Value of Competition. Before the age of two, children are likely not to respond to the motive of competion. Soon after that, however, an attitude of rivalry appears. By the age of six, as many as 80 per cent of all children appear to give evidence of competition when playing with blocks. Children seem to work harder in individual competition or as members of group against group than they do when the competitive aspect is eliminated. Competition for an individual can take on the form of competing with the record of another or of competing with his own record. The latter seems to be more sensible to the logically minded person, since the individual is competing on an equal basis with his own ability. Yet the intensity of competition is increased for most children when they are in situations in which they may compete with others in their group or in similar situations.

Use of Competition. The development of a competitive spirit is desirable when it is used wisely. It is harmful when the less able are placed in competition with the more able. When left to their own devices, children tend to select other children with whom they set their competitive goals. In school, unfortunately, this is likely to be the group at the head of the class. Teachers can make use of this principle if they are careful to pair off children of nearly equal ability or achievement in any learning area so that the children may experience a challenge to further learning.

Competition and Co-operation. There is an antithesis between competition and co-operation. Yet to engage in competitive activity does not imply the lack of co-operation. In fact, good competition cannot continue without the working relationship of co-operation in some of its phases. There is need for better balance between those who utilize competitiveness to a great extent and those who use it little as they seek to get ahead. Incentives should be provided so that competition will work for those who need it most rather than for those who need it least.

Undesirable behavior habits may result from too much emphasis upon competition in the classroom. In order to avoid failure or defeat, some children may resort to any means whether desirable or undesirable. They may cheat on a test, copy work from another child, prompt a young friend to enable the latter to excel, or otherwise exhibit behavior that is more or less dishonest. Attitudes of personal honor and integrity are difficult to engender when children engage in such practices.

IMPORTANCE OF DRIVES AND URGES

Every child exhibits inner drives that are dynamic forces. His thoughts, attitudes, emotions, and behavior are influenced by these drives as well as by the stimuli around him. His desirable adjustment to frustration can be measured in terms of the satisfaction or the thwarting of these urges and drives. Overt behavior is conditioned, controlled, or directed eventually by these inner drives as they come into interaction with the forces of the child's environment.

Some of the important inner drives and urges impel an individual to act in one or another way. The behavior in which he then engages brings about whatever frustration is developed when adjustment does not result. Some of these inner drives or urges that influence a child's behavior are the ones associated with bodily needs, success, superiority, recognition and approval, sympathy, security, and adventure.

Urges Associated with Bodily Needs. The urges for food and drink, protection, activity, sleep, and rest are biologically rooted drives that become so completely socialized in the child's life that they form a part of his cultural heritage. A child develops the habit of eating three times a day. He learns to like the food prepared by his mother, the water that he drinks, the clothes that he wears, and the bed in which he sleeps. If he is forced by circumstances to change his accustomed behavior, he may feel frustrated or even become quite disturbed.

In the fulfillment of these primitive impulses and needs, the child becomes sensitive to the customs of the society of which he rapidly is becoming a part. He wants to conform to the group pattern of behavior in the satisfying of these bodily urges. Attitudes in the group situation aid in effecting approved behavior. Clothing has value aside from the fact that it protects the child. The child who is called upon to wear hand-me-downs resists only when those in the situation tend to encourage values that should not be introduced. On his own, he is likely to be pleased with clothes that are clean and comfortable.

Urges Associated with the Behavior and Reactions of Others. The urges for success, superiority, recognition and approval, sympathy, security, and adventure have social implications for the child. The interactions brought about between the child and his associates through the force of these drive determine to a great extent the kind of adjustment he makes as he attempts to satisfy these drives.

Success. The feelings that accompany the successful completion of a project on which a child has worked for long hours are difficult to share with others. This success factor serves as a motivating force toward further development. The child who has experienced the satisfaction that goes with successful achievement is likely to be stimulated toward activity in another area in which he may be interested. The pleasure derived becomes a motivating force to stimulate similar attempts at other times and in other projects.

Superiority. The urge to be able to do something better than another person is valuable in child development. This drive is basic to individual success and happiness. A child craves activity and, even during the preschool years, he has a strong desire to excel. He is more interested in the fact that his production is better than that of another child to which he can compare his own than he is in the degree of its actual perfection.

If a child attempts to achieve superiority through socially unacceptable behavior, conflicts and frustrations are likely to occur. For example, one child may attempt to dominate group play by being more assertive in the expression of his opinion of the rules than is the child who is thoroughly acquainted with them. A feeling of inferiority is engendered in the latter by this more aggressive behavior of the former.

The urge for superiority is strong. Sometimes, to satisfy this urge the child cheats, lies, steals, or engages in some other form of subterfuge. This behavior is harmful to the individual as well as to the group. Too often a single breach of good behavior such as cheating in a test, stealing a pencil, or telling a falsehood labels a

127

child as a dishonest person. This reputation stays with him as long as he is a member of the group and may even spread to other groups, no matter how honest he may be in his general behavior. The effect upon the child of the one mistake may cause him to become emotionally embittered.

Recognition and Approval. A child craves attention. He exhibits the functioning of this urge in his early behavior. He seeks approval for his acts, and tends to play to the gallery. When he engages in an activity, he wants others to share it with him, and he observes keenly their attitude toward his achievement. A feeling of satisfaction accompanies the successful completion of a project in which he has participated. The pleasure is intensified when adults or others in the group give him approval and recognition.

The school child, failing to receive recognition and approval for his efforts, sometimes devises undesirable ways to attract the attention of the teacher and his classmates. He is especially interested in doing things that will gain the approval of his classmates, such as throwing a spit ball, operating a bean-shooter, or making faces behind the teacher's back, even though all these may get him into trouble with the teacher.

Behavior problems might be avoided if teachers would make wise use of praise and recognition of work that is well done. The parent or teacher should not follow a set plan in meting out praise but should attempt to evaluate each activity in terms of the ability of the child and the probable difficulties of achievement that the child may encounter. In this way, a child can be helped to develop a good sense of values.

Sympathy. A child likes to receive sympathetic attention from others. If he injures himself, the pain is alleviated when he realizes that others have sympathy for his suffering. Many of the little disappointments and frustrations of childhood may appear to the child to be great tragedies. The ill effects upon his emotions in such situations can be ameliorated if an understanding adult is symapthetic toward the child's discomfort but at the same time helps the child realize that the situation is only temporary.

Sympathy is sometimes solicited by a child. If he comes to feel that he is not receiving sufficient attention from his associates he may attempt to arouse their sympathy by an actual or imagined scratch, headache, or other sympathy-arousing condition. The display of this attitude is harmful to the child. If he receives the wanted attention he is likely thereby to develop habits of throwing himself on the mercy of others, instead of gaining their attention through desirable behavior. If he does not receive the desired attention, he may develop an attitude of self-pity and futility, to the detriment of his whole personality.

Security. As was said earlier, a child needs the feeling of security in the affection of his parents and of his other associates. A feeling of insecurity leads to maladjustment. The possession of this urge is one of the powerful socializing forces. In the child's drive to belong, he becomes agreeable to others and assumes as an attitude of give-and-take in the group situations in which he finds himself. He strives to keep in favor with the leader of the group.

Responsiveness to economic security enters the child's life only as he understands what that means. The time of such understanding varies with the attitudes displayed by family members and sometimes with the economic status of the family. This aspect of security is important in the emotional life of the child. The significance of this influence is indicated by the fact that to avoid insecurity men and women work long hours, women marry, men kill or rob, and millions subscribe to social security, pension systems, and insurance. During his later developmental years the child should come to recognize his responsibility for his own financial welfare, but during his early years he should not be stimulated to worry unduly about family finances.

Adventure. Curiosity or the urge to discover the new is normal. The child has numerous opportunities to give expression to this urge. During his early years he discovers many new things and has a strong urge to investigate them. If his activities are planned for him and are too rigidly supervised, he may feel frustrated in his desire to give expression to this drive. He enjoys building with blocks and tearing down what has been constructed. He thrills to the experience of prying into things and of investigating how this or that object is put together.

The child's spirit of adventure usually is satisfied easily. He turns quickly from one activity to another. However, if a child continues to be thwarted in his desire to experiment with the new and the different he may feel impelled to avoid dominating influences that curb his spirit of adventure. He may run away from home, he may become a truant, or he may become destructive or delinquent. This urge may dominate the behavior of an individual throughout his life and cause him to be dissatisfied with his status and living conditions, no matter how favorable these may be.

129

CHAPTER 10

Development of Social Behavior

Social stimuli influence a child from the time his life begins. Even before birth he exerts an influence upon those who are in his near surroundings. At first, he is relatively passive and remains so until the influence of other human beings upon him becomes more pronounced.

The child at birth is neither a social nor an unsocial being. He is capable of exerting a social influence and of being greatly affected by social stimuli from those about him. The helplessness of the human baby causes him to be dependent upon others for the fulfillment of his life needs. Although he is asocial at first, he does not long retain that status.

NATURE OF SOCIAL RESPONSES

There is an interweaving in social development all through an individual's life. The relationship can be thought of as personal-social. The individual exerts his influence on others while he is being influenced by them. As the associations with other human beings increase in number, social development progresses rapidly.

Relation to Other Factors. As an infant, and later an older child, depends upon others for the satisfaction of his needs, the ways in which these others meet his needs and his responses to their behavior become fundamental factors of social development. Social growth and development are closely linked with the physical, mental, and emotional aspects of development. The child's degree of other people's attitudes toward him and his physical wants. To the extent that his wants are met he responds with one or another form of emotional reaction. The child's reactions then are

130

interpreted rightly or wrongly in terms of the adult's degree of understanding, and one or another emotional attitude is aroused in the adult toward the child.

Social attitudes and behavior at any stage of development are affected directly by physiological conditions and changes, degree of mental alertness, and extent of emotional maturity as these are influenced by others or as they affect the behavior of others. Social habits are achieved in conjunction with these developing and maturing processes. If these social habits develop smoothly so that they can function satisfactorily in the child's social environment they produce the socially adaptable person who is equipped to meet adequately the various situations in which he finds himself.

Significance of Social Responses. Even among primitive peoples, group association was recognized to have value for both the individual and the group. One of a child's major responsibilities is to learn to adjust to the group or groups of which he is a member. The child's existence depends upon the society into which he is born. Eventually, he develops a personality that is patterned after its mores and folkways. As he grows, he learns that to be a good member of a group brings advantages to him. He also gradually recognizes what he must contribute to the welfare of the members of the group to advance either himself or the group.

The child is at the mercy of numerous social forces. During his prolonged infancy, he is being changed or molded by the stimuli in his social environment. Except in rare instances a human being does not live the life of a hermit. He has discovered that his greatest satisfactions come to him through the avenues of social living. The isolated life is both distasteful and unproductive.

The cultural heritage is needed by the child, and the existing culture needs him. Progress can be made only as the children of each generation build upon the social and cultural heritage of their day. The child is inducted into a certain kind of environment, and his interactions with this environment affect both himself and the factors of the environment. Human qualities continue to result from and are dependent upon association with other people.

STAGES OF SOCIAL DEVELOPMENT

As in other areas of development, the child's social progress is dependent upon the rate and kind of maturation that he experiences. Many differences can be found in the social patterns of children. Regardless of their degree of adequacy, social attitudes follow a relatively similar sequence of general development for most children.

Social Behavior during Infancy. Crying, smiling, and eye movement in response to others are forms of early social behavior. The perception of others is acquired by the infant as he is handled, bathed, and dressed by them. Before the age of three months the probably will show signs of social awareness such as fixing his eyes on his mother or nurse, smiling in response to her smile, or responding in other ways to her voice.

The crying and smiling of the neonate have no social significance. After about the third month, they are associated with people, especially those who care for the child's needs. Hence, crying and smiling now are beginning to take on characteristic forms of social behavior. Up to the age of five months the smile is a characteristic response regardless of the stimulus. Later the child begins to discriminate between approving or disapproving adult attitudes toward himself, and smiling and crying now represent the overt expression of the child's response to specific kinds of behavior on the part of those about him.

A study of the nature and extent of smiling among 139 male and 112 female babies, including white, Negro, and Indian infants, revealed that babies under twenty days of age did not smile and that not more than 2 per cent of these infants smiled before the age of two months. A smile was registered by 98 per cent of the group by the end of five months. It was found that motion of a person or object near the child acts as a stimulus for early smiling.

During his early months the baby also begins to give evidence of attempts to touch or to grasp others. The first signs of timidity or shyness in the presence of others may accompany the appearance of the ability to discriminate one person from another. At about the fifth or sixth month fear of strangers may be exhibited by the baby, although this may not always be the case. About this time the baby also may show a desire to be picked up. He may kick, coo, or laugh in order to attract attention to himself. During the latter part of his first year the child exhibits more overt signs of social behavior. He may explore the features of another person, grab a nose, or try to touch an object such as a chair or a watch. He makes playful advances to those whom he knows but may withdraw from strangers. After about ten months he can imitate movements such as clapping hands or shaking hand or head. He learns to participate

132

in social expression in such activities as peek-a-boo and waving bye-bye.

Co-operative play between children under one year of age seldom takes place. The baby may react to another young child in ways such as giving attention to the latter when he cries or attempting to exclude him from what may be considered a personal sphere of activity. The beginnings of social behavior in the one-year-old child are displayed in his many activities. He creeps, he attempts to walk, he picks up and throws objects and pushes them away, he plays with more facility, and, in general, he seems to have an interest in "getting into things" and the ability to do so.

The one-year-old child can understand the names of certain objects and can understand and obey certain definite commands. Up to this time he has been almost completely self-centered in his social relationships. He still needs and demands personal attention. His growing awareness of others, however, makes this a good time to start his training in the art of social living.

Laughter is a form of social behavior that comes into full swing at about the age of eighteen months to two years. Any simple little game will produce laughter in a baby. Before the age of two, he tends to laugh more when he is alone. Later, he laughs more in the presence of other children. It is easy to excite laughter in the pre-school child. The showing of a cartoon of the Walt Disney type may arouse gales of laughter.

Children of four or five months seldom are interested in children of the same age, as this interest is slow in dveloping. By fifteen or eighteen months the baby begins to play with another child but is likely to hit or bite the other, or try to obtain a toy that another child may want to take away from him. A social attitude toward his peers does not develop until later and even then may be slow in its formation. Sex differences do not play an important role in the social activities of the baby.

Social Development during the Nursery School and Kindergarten Period. The nursery school child wants to be considered as an individual. His behavior is indicative of the fact that he wants attention for himself. He looks upon things as his own and sometimes tries to take things from another for himself. This sets the stage for the development of other socializing attitudes. The child is given situational experiences that will enable him to discover right from wrong. His self-esteem is strengthened as he gradually learns to engage in activities with others of his own age level.

His capacity for group formation is still limited. Yet he shows an interest in games that include a few children. In the formation of groups for play either in the nursery school or kindergarten or in his home neighborhood a great deal of democracy is evidenced. When children are left to their own devices such factors as sex, race, color, or economic status do not influence them in the formation of their play groups.

Nursery school and kindergarten children look upon teachers as mother substitutes. This attitude may continue to show itself during the early years of elementary school life. Children need the demonstration of affection and the sense of security that they can experience with a teacher who is willing and able to exhibit a mother attitude toward them.

During this age period the child in the home is relatively self-centered. When he goes to nursery school or kindergarten he encounters situations that in their social aspect are very different from those to which he has been accustomed. The child should not be kept a baby too long, but neither should he be expected to become self-reliant and socially minded before he is prepared for these changes in behavior. He must be led gradually to shift from his interest in his former imaginary playmates to willingness to enter into social activities with real children of his own age. The child who has played with other children in his home neighborhood prior to his entrance into the nursery school or kindergarten finds this transition relatively easy.

Social Development during the Elementary School Years. The child in the primary grades of the elementary school still is individualistic, especially if he has not had the experiences of social development that are found in the nursery school and kindergarten. In the modern school he encounters the kind of social activities that help him to learn to share with others and to co-operate with others in his work and play. All these social activities need to be carefully even though indirectly planned, organized, and supervised by teachers who know what to expect in social development at each age level.

During the ages from six to ten, the child exhibits progressively in his behavior, either desirable or undesirable, his growing recognition of himself in relation to other people. His attitudes toward others are likely to be influenced by whatever urge, desire, or interest is present at the moment. His whole emotional pattern is such that he often does things that appear to have no reasonable basis for their doing.

In his relations with his teacher, he may respect and like him or her. But he cannot resist his impulse to tease. As an expression of his urge to free himself from what to him may appear to be teacher domination he may joke about the teacher in whispers, draw unflattering pictures on the board or at his seat, or in many other ways indicate that the teacher is his natural enemy. Such behavior is not an indication of fundamental antagonism, but rather one of the signs of developing self-realization.

Unsupervised, the child may yell, throw chalk, or chase another child around the room or playground. At the same time he displays strong loyalties that to the adult may seem to be more or less unreasonable. His father is the greatest man in town; his teacher is better than any other teacher in school; his class is brighter than any other class; his school wins more honors than any other school.

The children begin to form groups of their own. Some of these play groups are more or less temporary at first. After nine or ten years of age, however, many children seem to want to belong to and become an acceptable member of a particular club or social group. Group pressures tend to provide the necessary social drive to cause most members to conform to the rules and regulations of the group. Social approval is coveted and sought openly.

Toward the end of this period, children become very much interested in hobbies. Sex differences that have begun to show themselves in other areas of social activities are evidenced in the kinds of hobbies engaged in by boys and girls, respectively. In an extensive survey of the hobbies of sixth grade children, it was found that not only was there a difference between the sexes but also in levels of intelligence. The higher the intelligence the more likely was interest in hobbies to be present. For example, collecting was prominent among both boys and girls. Boys evinced great interest in history, science, and biography, and girls in playing musical instruments.

ASPECTS OF THE SOCIALIZING PROCESS

The process of socialization takes many forms. A few of these appear to exercise a potent influence upon a child's personality. A child's relationship with others may be friendly or antisocial. He may be motivated by the spirit of competition or by a desire to cooperate. Each of these phases of social interrelations follows a generally uniform sequential pattern of development, except insofar as innate characteristics or environmental influences affect a child's social behavior at any stage of his progress toward the attainment of social maturity.

Friendship among Children. Strong attachments may occur between two children at the ages of three or four. These usually are of short duration, perhaps no more than a few days, although they may last for years. If the friendship is between two children only, one of them usually dominates the other. At times, however, the situation is reversed and the follower becomes the leader. Too great an attachment between two children of this age may interfere with the development of desirable social relationships with other children. Hence, other children should be brought into the situation who can modify, to some extent, any undesirable effects that may be inherent in the two some relationship.

Children form their friendships in much the same way as do adults. Age or growth status is more important, however, with children than it is with adults. Children tend to form their friendships in terms of age or school-grade status, intelligence, extent of sociability, or resemblance to a child of previous acquaintance. Sometimes the friendship may result from a chance meeting in which similarity in interests or attitudes is discovered.

The difficulties of a new child entering a group are many. He may not always be received at first by the children with whom he wishes to associate himself. One child, however, may give him attention. The new child is grateful for this attention and as a result accepts the other as his friend. The situation may become awkward if later he is accepted by the desired group but the other child is excluded from it. He is then torn between his loyalty to his first friend in the new situation and the group into which he has been accepted. He may resolve the conflict by withdrawing himself from both, by attempting to remain friends with both, or by persuading the group to accept his friend.

A deliberate effort to win friends is good training in social living. The child who seems to have no particular friend among the children of a group needs adult help in the making of friends. If he is left to his own clumsy devices he may antagonize rather than attract. This often happens to the bright child who in the home has been encouraged to show his superiority.

136

Children find their friends in the home environment from among the children of their parents' associates, and in the school or a neighborhood playground. Young children show no preference as to sex. After the first year of the elementary school they seem to select as their best friends members of the same sex. School companions may or may not continue their social activities together during after-school hours.

Quarrels and Fights among Children. Bickering and quarreling characterize the behavior of some children as they make their adjustments in group living. The egocentric behavior of a child does not give way without a struggle to the outgoing attitudes and behavior that must develop as he transfers complete interest in self to interest in others. In group behavior the self-centered desires and urges clash. One child wants what he sees another child have; he wants to be where the other child is. He may deliberately bump into another or enter into physical combat.

A child's aggressive attitude toward another child is normal and may serve various purposes. Quarreling or tussling may strengthen the bond of friendship if it is done with a play attitude and is between two good friends. When an emotional antagonism is aroused toward a child who is not a close friend, quarreling and tussling are not socializing influences. This form of aggressive attitude may have its roots in jealousy or may be caused by antisocial attitudes toward the child who seems to be the aggressor in the quarrel or fight. Boys tend to engage in physical combat as an emotional outlet. Although a girl may pull another girl's hair, girls usually quarrel vocally.

Competition and Co-operation. The many various feelings and actions of which a child is capable in relation to other people are not fundamentally negative and antisocial, but rather are they positive and desirable. The early behavior of an infant is neither competitive nor co-operative. To excel is not a part of his understanding experience during the first few weeks of life.

Bases of Competition. The baby soon learns to experience jealousy toward a rival for the affection of his parents. Also, a two- or three-year-old child perhaps is bigger than he is, or the other's plaything seems more attractive than his. An experience of this kind may be intolerable for the young child. His consequent jealous behavior may take on any one of various forms. There are large differences among children in their sensitivity to aggression.

Before the age of three, however, competitiveness does not affect

137

the child's behavior very much. A child usually plays with his blocks, unmindful of what another child may be doing with other blocks. As he is affected more and more by his cultural patterns he begins to exhibit competition as well as co-operation in achievement.

A child's show of aggressive behavior may be the result of his social experiences after he is sufficiently mature to understand unfavorable comparisons. The presence of this attitude is shown by his disposition to behave aggressively in situations that affect his security as regards people who mean something to him or his prized possessions. A friend may excel in achievement without arousing displeasure, but if an unfriendly rival surpasses him, aggressive attitudes will be exhibited. A child may show competition in one situation and none or little in another. The difference in his behavior is caused by the extent to which he is interested in a person, object, or game.

The elementary school child usually is interested in self-advancement. He works for individual honor. Interest in group activity is not keen unless rivalry has been stimulated, perhaps by an adult, between a group of which he is a member and another group. Then the members of each group will band together to maintain the honor of their side. This is one of the values of interscholastic debate, baseball, or football, if the rivalry is not carried too far. Group cooperation can be strengthened through a unifying of the efforts and loyalties that are inherent in the situation.

Co-operative Behavior. Co-operative effort can be stimulated in the child more easily than some adults seem to realize. Fundamentally, a child seeks approval. Not only is he willing to be helpful in order to merit commendation, but he also begins to recognize the fact that older children and adults receive social approval when they do things for one another.

If or when a child seems to be unco-operative, there usually is a real reason for his attitude. A task assigned to him may be too difficult. He may know that he is supposed to do something, but he does not quite know what it is or how he should do it. The request or the directions may have been given on the adult's level of understanding rather than the child's.

Another reason for a child's not co-operating may be that his childish interest in another form of activity may be so strong at the moment that it is intolerable to him to change it. It even may be that he does not feel well, although he does not yet show any outward signs of illness. The example of unco-operative behavior among his associates also may influence his degree of willingness to co-operate, since he is a great imitator. Unless an adult dealing with an apparently unco-operative child can recognize the possible bases of such behavior he may regard the child as stubborn or bad-tempered. He may punish the child or deny him privileges. Such treatment does little more than intensify the child's unco-operative attitude and build up deep resentments in him.

FACTORS INFLUENCING SOCIAL DEVELOPMENT

Attention has been directed in the foregoing to the fact that the development of social maturity is dependent upon the nature of the child and the ways in which environmental factors affect his growing self.

Emotions and Social Development. The emotion-arousing nature of many stimuli in the child's environment exerts a powerful influence upon the social values developed by him. Since the experience backgrounds of children and adults differ, similar stimuli do not arouse emotions of like intensity in both at the same time. Yet in many situations the emotional qualities of a child's experience are the direct results of those experienced by his parents and others around him.

Emotional and social expansion go together. By observing others, especially his ideal, the child is motivated to imitate them in what he does and in the way he expresses himself. Social values are achieved in great part from the example of others.

It is emotionally disturbing to a child if parents or other leaders are not consistent in their demands or in their methods of control. A child is confused when his mother, who has been teaching him not to tell a lie, is heard by him as she tells a "little white lie" in order to avoid embarrassment either to herself or to another person. He cannot understand that there may be a difference between his mother's lie and the untruth that he tells to protect his own ego or self-respect.

Leadership and Social Development. Leadership traits begin to show themselves in the kindergarten, if not earlier. They are manifestations of the dominance of one child over another and may be expressed in a variety of ways. The young leader may be larger in size, he may be more vocal, or he may be able to run faster than the other children. The leader in a game may be the one who knows best how to play the game. Another child may lead as a result of his skill in establishing friendly relations with other children. A child who is aggressive may force leadership through his coercieve methods.

The power of the leadership drive differs among children. A child can or is willing to give leadership in one situation and not in another. A leader who is chosen by his group has advantages of group and individual co-operation which are not always experienced by a leader who has been superimposed upon a group. This is the chief reason for allowing children to select their own classroom, school, or game leaders whenever possible.

Friction sometimes develops among children because each member of a group wants to be the leader. Hence, a child should be helped to understand that he sometimes must follow the lead of someone else. He may be a leader in one group or situation but should be a follower of a good leader in another group.

Many quarrels among children result from the desire to be a leader. Sometimes a group selects one of its members to be a leader and then finds that he does not have leadership qualities, since he cannot understand the desires of the other children and do something to satisfy them. In any school or play situation a child may be found who is usually chosen by his associates to lead their activities. He is the self-confident child who is willing and able to inspire the group and to establish favorable emotional attitudes among the members of the group.

Play Activities and Social Behavior. Through play, the child gives expression to his impulses and to behavior that is social in nature. Through play, also, a child reveals the kind of young person he is. As he plays with other children, a child displays his kind and degree of imagination, his ability to co-operate, and his sense of fair play.

Adult manners, standards, and ways of thinking are reflected in the play of children. The play attitude is valuable in all aspects of development and is pertinent especially to desirable social development. Most of a child's play is engaged in with other children in one or another form of relatively free activity. Hence, the child is enabled through play to learn to submerge his egocentric urges and wishes.

Play affects every age group and differs with the age group. During early childhood, boys and girls tend to participate together in their play activities. Later, their interests differ. This difference can be explained partly by the fact that boys are stronger than girls and partly by the earlier maturing of girls and the cultural pressures that affect both the play behavior and the recreational activities of girls.

The choice of play associates depends upon many factors. These include economic status, type of neighborhood, and intellectual level. The bright child tends to select an older child as a playmate, and a dull child may need to play with younger children, since the children of his own age will not accept him as a playmate.

Some parents are overcautious about their child's playmates. This child may then find it difficult to make a satisfactory adjustment to other children and is likely to build his outlet for approval and recognition in the world of fantasy and daydreaming. Inadequate experience with other children leaves the child unsocialized. He is likely to become the shy, moody, and jealous child who is suspicious of the behavior of others. He has been denied opportunities to develop the skill of meeting and dealing with his peers. Social adjustment comes to the child only through continued social experiences.

Clubs, Gangs, and Camp Experiences. Most children are gregarious. They want to be included in peer groups, even though they may participate in only a minor way in the activites of the group. Also, although a normal child who is secure in the affection of adults, such as his parents and teachers, is amenable to the general pattern of social living to which he is oriented by adults, he still needs opportunities to express his social interests without too close supervision. This is especially true of the child of later elementary school years or older.

The young child gradually attaches himself to play groups in his immediate neighborhood. With other members of such groups, he usually engages in more or less informal play activities. Sooner or later he experiences the urge for membership in a more definite group or club composed of his peers. He wants to help to plan, organize, and carry out projects that are associated with his growing interests and that are directed toward the realization of a specific goal. Whether this goal is desirable from the adult point of view is not particularly important to the young person. Hence, it is the responsibility of adults to provide constructive opportunities for group activities and to encourage the child's participation in those activities. Many formally organized and wholesome groups are now available.

Availability of Clubs. National and international organizations such as the Boy Scouts, the Girl Scouts, the Camp Fire Girls, the "Y's," and the Four-H clubs have been popular because young people need a kind of organization in which or through which they can express themselves without too much adult supervision. These organizations, good as they are, are not sufficient in number to provide opportunities to all children and young people for social expression.

Gang Influences. The block group is still one of the important agencies of the social life of children and young people. Such groups are prominent in most urban communities and may develop into a relatively if not completely undesirable "gang" situation. The gang may formulate its own codes and use undesirable quarters as a meeting place. In time, the members of a gang may get into difficulty with themselves, with other citizens, and sometimes with the law.

Gangs usually thrive in communities where boys are thrown on their own resources to find social stimulation. Gangs organize to solve their own problems. Some of the gangs that are active in the more congested urban areas are responsible for acts of juvenile delinquency. Although gangs may exist in less congested areas, the activities of these gangs usually do not exercise so undesirable an effect upon their members, chiefly perhaps because the young people are willing to accept some adult supervision of their activities.

Value of Camp Life. An increasing number of boys and girls are being afforded an opportunity to engage in healthful recreational and social experiences through camp activities. At camp, the child expresses himself with his peers in healthful surroundings. He is not entirely free from supervision, but the wide open spaces of the camp allow for a feeling of freedom to develop outgoing social attitudes as he lives and plays with his peers.

Camp life encourages the development of independence and self-confidence. There is value to the child in learning to live away from his parents for a short time and to do those things for himself which at home usually are done for him by the parents. Sending a child to camp has value for the parents also. They must learn sooner or later that they are not completely necessary in the life of the child. The yearly camp experience provides a proving ground for the accomplishment of this important objective. Not only are parents giving attention to camp life for their children, but also boards of education are experimenting with ways to raise money to carry out these educational experiences as part of the school life of children and young people.

CHAPTER 11

Character Development and Discipline

A child is born into a culture in which certain moral standards or ethical principles have been developed. These standards or principles are the ones generally accepted by the members of the group as behavior guides so that their kind of civilization may be preserved or improved.

SIGNIFICANCE OF CHARACTER

Every culture demands that the people follow accepted patterns of behavior. Various terms are used to describe the individual's relationship to the accepted mode of behavior.

Morality. The term *morality* signifies adherence to the moral code of the group, i.e., conformity in behavior to the manners or customs of the social group. The moral person conforms. The immoral person engages in behavior that is regarded as detrimental to the general welfare. Unmoral or amoral behavior, in contrast to immoral behavior, represents conduct that is regarded as unfavorable to the general good but that is engaged in from ignorance of what is expected rather than motivated by the deliberate intention to break the code.

Ethics. Ethical understanding is supposed to be an individual's recognition of the difference between right and wrong. Whether these terms are interpreted as absolute or as relative, the newborn child becomes a member of a society that has set for itself certain ideals of conduct which the child will be expected to recognize and to observe in his social behavior.

Character. The terms *personality* and *character* sometimes are used together to describe an individual's total pattern of reaction.

144

Personality is interpreted by some as including *character*. More generally, however, *personality* has a psychological connotation as representing the development of all an individual's physical, mental, emotional, and social traits. *Character* applies specifically to those attitudes and behavior responses that affect his welfare or the welfare of other members of his group, as these are regarded as right or wrong.

The Child as a Moral Being. Various beliefs have been held concerning the nature of the child at birth. Some of these are: (1) the child is born in sin and his innate depravity must be driven out of him by strict disciplinary measures; (2) the newborn child is pure but loses his purity through contact with the wicked ones of the world; (3) the child is born with a conscience that enables him from birth onward to distinguish between right and wrong — he has inherited a sense of moral values.

The truth of the matter probably is that the newborn child is neither moral nor immoral, but rather amoral. At birth, he possesses certain potentialities of behavior and disposition. In terms of the inner and outer factors of influence that he will experience during his developmental years, these will determine the kind of person he eventually will become as a member of his group.

STAGES IN THE DEVELOPMENT OF CHARACTER

As has been shown in earlier chapters, the infant soon comes to respond to elements in his environment. By smiles and frowns he gives evidence of pleasantness and unpleasantness. By the time he is twelve weeks old there appears to be a give-and-take in smiling that seems to indicate that intersocial relations are beginning to be established. From then on, the young child progressively learns what is expected of him and, for the most part, attempts to respond accordingly.

The child's early attempts to behave in an acceptable manner have no basis in moral discrimination. He cannot understand broad ethical concepts. His responses are specific and in terms of specific situations. Approval of his conduct is satisfying, disapproval is annoying. As he grows older, such terms as *goodness* and *badness, obedience* and *disobedience,* and *honesty* and *dishonesty* may be included in his developing verbal vocabulary. These ethical or moral concepts have little or no meaning for him, except as he experiences them in specific situations.

The First Three Years. During the earliest years, the egocentric child regards his experiences in terms of his own satisfaction. His responses are impulsive, although he seems to recognize certain adult words or gestures to be admonitions to him to change his behavior. By the end of his first year he enjoys engaging in behavior that will earn for him expressions of adult approval.

During his second and third years, the child may run away and drop an object that he should not have taken. He blames inanimate objects or other people for unpleasant happenings to himself, and becomes angry if his wishes are thwarted. At about two years, he learns to repeat phrases such as "good boy" and "bad boy" as describing his way of eating, toilet routines, and the like.

By the time a child has reached the age of thirty months, his behavior appears to be motivated by an urge to do what he wants to do, at his own time and in his own way. His favorite response to an adult request is a defnite "No," a shake of the head, or other unco-operative gestures. This period of development is referred to as the *negativistic* stage. It is interesting to note, however, that the child actually may do what is asked of him at the same time that he is giving vehement expression to his unwillingness to do so.

If handled patiently and intelligently, the child usually emerges from the period of apparent nonco-operation with an increased understanding of what constitutes desirable behavior. Although he continues to pattern his behavior in terms of his own interests, he attempts to do right things and avoid wrong acts because he has come to appreciate the satisfactions to himself that accompany his receiving adult approval, and the annoying effects upon himself of adult disapproval.

The child has not yet recognized the ethical aspect of behavior. This attitude is exemplified by his interest in possession. During his second year he usually develops a fondness for one or more special toys, such as a woolly dog or a doll. He wants it with him at all times, even in bed. This attitude gradually spreads toward all his toys. He will not share them with other children. Although he seems to know what belongs to whom in the home, he is likely to pick up anything that strikes his fancy outside the home.

By the time he is two and one-half years old, the urge to possess impels him to take as his own for his own play activity anything that is within reach, although he may soon tire of it. Nothing is safe around the house — he will take ornaments, pots and pans, and similar reachable, graspable, and manipulatable objects. He also

146

begins to become interested in the possession of pennies, which he hoards and exhibits to others as he does his other possessions.

Toward the end of his third year, the child begins to show some recognition of the rights of others. He may share his toys, and he is not so prone to take what does not belong to him. He realizes that money is something with which he can buy things, but he has no conception of relative money value. He also shows greater understanding of what is meant by good or bad behavior, although his life still centers around himself and his wants. Modification of these egocentric attitudes can be brought about through adult example and patient adult training.

Later Preschool Years. Between the ages of three and six years, the child makes considerable progress in his appreciation of himself as a social entity. He still tends to conform to expected behavior standards in terms of approval or disapproval. He is still amoral, but he recognizes the fact that there are certain rules that should govern his behavior. If he obeys these rules he is good; when he disobeys them he is naughty. He does not understand adult-made rules and regulations, but neither does he question them.

The child may resent restrictions of desired activity. He may try to evade punishment for wrongdoing. Some of his techniques for doing this are: to try to hide a broken toy or other object, to place the blame for his naughtiness on another person or even on an inanimate object, and to excuse his behavior as an accident or as not intended. These evasions or alibis are not expressions of the child's recognition of moral values, however, but grow out of his reluctance to suffer punishment for his wrongdoing. Any expressions of contriteness or remorse are, for the most part, merely verbal rather than the overt expression of inner repentance.

Specifically, the child progresses in his behavior responses in his relation to his environment. He is proud of his parents, of his home, and of his special possessions. If he is attending nursery school or kindergarten, he likes to boast of his family and to take his prized possessions to school where he may share them with other children. He sometimes forgets to bring these things home with him after he has exhibited them. He also likes to exchange toys with his special friends. He wants to have pets. Although he seems willing to share in caring for them he is likely to be foregetful.

He has not yet achieved a working concept of honesty, as illustrated by his tendency to carry home small articles. It may be difficult for him to distinguish between fact and fiction since he lives in two worlds — real and imaginary. Hence, he is given to the telling of stories that have little basis in fact.

As the child nears his sixth birthday, he may become more destructive of his toys and other objects because his curiosity about them causes him to take them apart to discover what is inside. He likes to collect many different things and is still proud of his possessions but is less boastful about them. He is careless about his possessions; he either breaks or loses them. He now begins to take things because he wants them for his own use rather than to add to his collection of possessions. He still may indulge in imaginative stories and the telling of falsehoods but shows some recognition of their deviation from reality and truth.

Elementary School Years. Studies of children's attitudes toward law and order seem to reveal that by the time children reach their twelfth year their attitudes gradually have approached those of adults. During the period of growth, they develop some understanding of general concepts of morality or of ethical principles.

The standards of group behavior with which the child attains at least a verbal acquaintance reflect the principles of conduct that govern the behavior of his adult and peer associates. He also gains the ability to discriminate to some extent between what might be considered to be desirable or undesirable in different situations. His power of judgment concerning moral values depends upon his degree of development of reasoing and judgment in general.

The elementary school child who in his rearing has been exposed to considerable emphasis upon moral generalization may become what has been described by some as a "self-righteous little prig." Whether that term should be applied to him is questionable. He does seem to exhibit a strong feeling about honesty and justice. Verbally, at least, he condemns lying, stealing, cheating, hurting small animals or younger children, and telling tales. As he now is passing through the gang period, his standards are those of his group and he usually shows rigidity of attitude toward the behavior of children outside the gang.

The child's own behavior may or may not reflect his verbalized attitudes. His conduct often is based upon expediency or the impulse of the moment. He has not yet (if he ever does) consciously set up standards of behavior that can be termed true morality and that will inhibit him from wrongdoing. He still fears the consequences of engaging in disapproved behavior activities.

148

He may consider a certain form of behavior wrong in one situation but not in another. He learns to obey one member of the family or one teacher more quickly than another. He may engage in selfish or unmannerly behavior in the home but refrains from such conduct in the school. He may have still another mode of behavior among his peers associates. In other words, the child may develop a double or even a triple set of standards by which his behavior is motivated in terms of what he considers most satisfying to himself.

The progress of the child's character-formation during later childhood shows a gradual development from a less social to a more social stage. At the age of six the child associates goodness and badness with specific situations, and he is not always responsive to the criticism of elders when he is naughty. He may regard their request or demand as unfair. At the same time he may criticize the naughty acts of his little friends and report such acts to others. He tells falsehoods to avoid punishment for his misdeeds and may cheat in games. He likes to have pennies to spend for candy or small articles but cares nothing about saving money. He may take things that interest him but rarely steals pennies.

The seven- and eight-year-old child gradually becomes aware of goodness or badness as something that is not tied immediately to a situation. He wants to be good and have his goodness appreciated. He begins to suffer remorse for acts of naughtiness and wants to be forgiven when he does something wrong. He still dislikes to admit that what he has done is wrong, but he seems to desire to live up to the standards of his parents and other adults.

The child at this age is very much interested in collecting things of interest to himself. He hoards them, takes great pride in them, and wants his own special place to keep them, but he may not take good care of them. Boys continue to be untidy about their clothes; girls are much more dress-conscious and usually are neat in appearance.

Money has come to have a significant meaning for the child in terms of what it can get for him. He wants an allowance and may do odd jobs around the house to earn extra money. He may save some of this money to purchase for himself a relatively expensive article, such as a baseball bat, a bicycle, or a particular article of dress.

Lying is less frequent, except as the child exaggerates in order to impress others. He usually recognizes his departues from the truth, however. He tends to be truthful in situations that to him seem important, and is very much concerned about the behavior of his friends in matters of honesty.

Preadolescent Years. The child from nine to twelve years of age begins to exhibit those character traits that he is likely to continue during his adolescent and adult years. His standards of conduct are influenced to a great extent by those of his group. He gradually develops concepts of rightness and wrongness in general and of specific aspects of desirable behavior. His growing self-consciousness in group situations impels him to be careful of the effect of his conduct upon others. He still is impulsive, though, and deviates from his own established code. He is much concerned about these deviations and may experience extreme embarrassment and remorse, sometimes to the point of trying to "make good" in his behavior so that he again may earn the good will of his associates.

The preadolescent continues to maintain high standards of conduct for his young friends but is less likely to report their misdoings. The attitude may show itself in the form of contempt for or even ostracism of another child who "peaches" or tattles on a friend.

More discrimination in the selection of possessions and in the care of them is evidenced. Money has definite significance and may be used to purchase gifts for others as well as to satisfy personal wants. Rarely does the twelve-year-old consciously set out to take things that belong to others, although he may do this impulsively or thoughtlessly.

In general, by the time the child enters his adolescent years, he has achieved a fairly responsible attitude toward his personal and social obligations. He is not yet mature, however. His verbal concepts of moral values are not always reflected in his behavior. He cannot always understand the relationship between adult admonitions to him concerning his conduct and adult behavior as observed by him. In some instances, he is very much confused by divergences between the two, and is influenced in his own behavior by adult example rather than adult precept. He has not yet set up completely a set of ethical standards which can be expected to function adequately for him in all situations, but he has progressed a long way from the egocentric bases of behavior which dominated in his early childhood.

FACTORS INFLUENCING CHARACTER DEVELOPMENT

Moral or ethical behavior must be learned. At first through imitation and later by means of more or less conscious effort, the child acquires attitudes and behavior patterns as he interacts with the individuals who constitute his environment and is affected by other factors of it. The home and the members of the family group probably are the most important factors of influence. Other influences include those of the school and church, and peer associates. The child's developing character also is molded by many elements inherent in modern community life, such as reading material, motion pictures, radio and television, and other recreational facilities.

The Home. The child's behavior is influenced not only by the family's attitude toward and treatment of himself but also by the attitudes displayed by the various members of the family toward one another, their behavior in the home, and their relationships to persons and things outside the home.

Parents' Attitudes toward the Child. Much has been written concerning the effect upon a child of being a wanted or a rejected child. The effect upon a child of his parents' attitudes toward him depends not so much upon whether they wanted him as it does upon their understanding of his needs and their ability to meet these needs in all areas of his developing personality. To the extent of such understanding and ability, he will be enabled to progress through the various stages of interpersonal relationships until he obtains a comprehension of his social as well as personal responsibilities and obligations.

Home Conditions. Conditions favorable to desirable adjustment are experienced by the child who is reared in a home in which kindliness, sincerity, honesty, and co-operation are practiced daily by the other members of the family. It is difficult for a young person to develop outgoing attitudes if his growing years are spent with a family whose members are likely to engage in bickering and quarreling, to be inconsiderate, or to give evidence of dishonest, self-centered, or unfair practices in their relationships with people outside the home.

Other factors that may militate against a child's experiencing a favorable home environment include continued illness of one or more members of the family, and subnormal intelligence of parents. Low economic status also tends to have an unfavorable

151

effect, although this is not necessarily so. A "poor" home is not necessarily a bad home. The child is affected adversely, however, by unhealthful living conditions, lack of cleanliness, undesirable ways of living, and a family attitude of bitterness and discontent arising out of meager living.

Many studies have been made of the effects upon children of an unfavorable home environment. Results of these studies indicate that children reared in such homes are more likely than other children to be either overaggressive or unduly submissive in their reltaions with others, to steal, to lie, to bully, to run away from home, or to engage in generally unacceptable behavior. Home conditions seem to have significance in cases of juvenile delinquency, especially among girls.

The School. As a child's social environment is enlarged to include interrelationships with teachers and schoolmates, the behavior habits and attitudes he has acquired to this point are either intensified or modified. His experiences in concrete school situations that encourage the development of desirable group behavior can serve as effective means of improving his attitudes and of helping him to gain greater understanding of general concepts of morality or of ethical principles.

Through the media of sports, pupil government, and group projects, the child learns attitudes of good sportsmanship, co-operation, and intelligent citizenship. Care needs to be taken, however, by school personnel so that the child does not develop, at the same time, habits of cheating and other dishonest forms of behavior that may result from too great or unsuitable competition.

Peer Associates. The very young child is not affected significantly by children of the same age even though they are in his immediate environment. Beginning with his attendance in nursery school, peer associates are likely to have an influence upon the child's behavior that is intensified on the elementary school level as he becomes a member of groups or gangs of children.

The influence of playmates upon a child's attitudes may be strong enough for him to develop aggressive behavior that is counter to parental rule. This is especially true if the group leader is a child whose home training is different from that of a group follower. The follower may experience conflict as he attempts to abide by parental regulations and at the same time maintain status in the group.

DISCIPLINE IN RELATION TO CHARACTER-BUILDING

Traditionally, discipline has referred to control of the child's behavior by forces outside himself. Today, more emphasis is placed upon the inner drives that activate a child's behavior. The external, authoritarian approach afforded little if any opportunity for the child to develop inner strength or the power to make decisions on his own. Rigid discipline was likely to arouse a constant conflict between his attempts to conform to group mores and customs and his desire for freedom of action and expression.

Meaning of Self-discipline. The parent does not always realize that a child is not a bundle of inherent badness but that he is ready to behave in situations as he is trained or disciplined. Self-control is one of the most important aspects of character development. The child learns that he cannot live in a social situation without reacting to the habits, thinking patterns, and general attitudes of the members of his group. He must adjust to them as they in turn adjust to him.

A child cannot be expected to attain, unaided, a satisfactory control of his behavior. He develops, in his home, conduct patterns that will benefit or harm him in his later social relationships. The factors of discipline concern the child for his own welfare, but they also affect others since his rights end at the point where the rights of another begin. Hence, from infancy onward he must be helped to learn that he should not initiate any form of activity that may interfere with the approved activity of others in his group. As a child comes to direct his behavior in terms of an understanding of his responsibility for the welfare of others as well as for his own, he is developing self-control or self-discipline.

Self-discipline implies the establishment within the child of many behavior patterns that will enable him or her to live and associate more effectively with other persons and be at peace with himself or herself. These habit patterns then become the motivating forces that give positive direction to the thinking and behavior of the individual as he or she lives and grows. It provides strong desires for the child to display behavior that is in conformity with that which is best for him or her as well as for others.

Self-discipline includes the formation of those behavior patterns which enables the child gradually to eliminate those forms of behavior patterns that may tend to militate against his or her own happiness as each strives for social growth, social acceptance, and self-fulfillment. In other words, self-discipline manifests itself as the individual acquires self-control and respect toward others in a social situation.

Many psychologists and educators believe that a self-disciplined child is one who has achieved the kind of self-control that enables him or her to function well in any social situation. The child has developed those behavior patterns and habits which serve him or her well and, at the same time, prevent his or her behavior from interfering with the welfare of others. The child then has achieved an inner satisfaction that functions in his or her life and displays the kind of behavior that is good for him or her and for those with whom he or she associates.

Types of Disciplinary Problems. Many situations experienced by a child contain what may be referred to as disciplinary elements. The following are some of the problems that confront him during his early years and that need parental help toward their solution.

Refusal to eat	Dawdling
Careless toilet habits	Lying
Bed-wetting	Stealing
Masturbation	Deliberate property damage
Thumb-sucking	Cruelty to animals
Nail-biting	Neglecting home chores
Temper tantrums	Doing things without permission
Carelessness	Misbehaving in school
Noisiness	Disinterest in school work
Roughness at play	Overinterest in play
Fights and quarrels	Impertinence
Profanity	Stubbornness
Obscenity	Staying up late

Teachers also are alert to definite types of problems that show themselves in the overt behavior of children. Some common types of these problems are as follows.

Tardiness	Physical attack
Truancy	Extreme timidity
Restlessness	Vandalism
Whispering in class	Name-calling
Writing notes in class	Cheating
Poor school work	Smoking
Profanity	Drinking
Temper tantrums	Gambling
Defiance of authority	Puppy-love behavior

These problems do not all represent the same degree of seriousness. The overt expression of some may represent no more than bad manners or thoughtlessness. Habitual or deliberate misbehavior becomes a serious problem and needs correction while the child still is in his formative stage. Sometimes behavior problems are rooted in emotional disturbances. If they are not curbed they may persist and become basic to later antisocial behavior or attitudes.

Types of Disciplinary Measures. An expanding number of measures is being used in the home for the treatment of childish misbehavior. In the past, spanking or other forms of corporal punishment were common. Results of studies show that parents are becoming less prone to use physical coercion for the purpose of conditioning a child's behavior. Other formerly used methods also are being discarded. These include such practices as to put a child into a dark room or send him to bed, to separate the child from the group, to bribe him, or to ridicule him. More commonly used techniques at present include: reasoning with the child, removing him from a temptation-arousing situation, substituting other activities for the disapparoved one, praising desirable conduct, giving the child considerable freedom in his activities, and depriving him of a possession or a special privilege.

More and more parents attempt to reason with the child, showing him in language suited to his understanding what the consequences of his misbehavior may be. For example, a father discovered his five-year-old son carrying a book of matches from the home to a neighboring wood. The child admitted that he and his friends intended to set fire to a pile of brushwood that they had collected. Instead of becoming emotionalized, the father demonstrated to the child the danger of fire by lighting the book of matches and throwing it quickly into a near-by pan of water. The father then explained to the child that his hand could have been burned badly if he had held on to the lighted matches. Thus the seriousness of fire hazards was made clear to the child in a concrete situation. No one method of instruction, however, fits every situation.

Development of Self-discipline. Behavior practiced in the home tends to set up within the individual child certain specific habit patterns that make for desirble relationships with other people. When these begin to operate without the domination of another's influence, the child is giving evidence of the qualities of self-discipline.

One or more forms of discipline need to be utilized in order to help a child develop self-control. He responds early to punishment of his misdeeds. He also must learn to respond to fair rules and regulations, and to authority and dominance used reasonably by others.

Rules and Regulations. Since the achievement of self-discipline is an exceedingly complex and difficult task, children should be provided with achievable rules or regulations as conduct guides. These rules of behavior should be formulated for the protection of the child and of his associates. They should not represent the whims of a person in authority.

For good democratic living, each child should be sensitive to the rules (codes of behavior) of society and be stimulated to live by them without external pressure or compulsion. A parent, a teacher, or a policeman is needed to insure fair play for everyone concerned so that each can be granted an equal freedom of activity.

Role of Authority. At birth, a child's potentialities for expression are unorganized. Qualitative behavior is learned in accordance with opportunities for dynamic, creative social living. The child's purposeful activity must be guided by the parent, teacher, or other adult who can give suggestions for and direction to his behavior. These adults must have achieved the status of knowing the rules, practicing them, and being willing to help the child live by them. This does not mean that the child may not sometimes engage in spontaneous experimental behavior.

A child should not be expected to give automatic responses to commands to those in authority. The attempt to give a child freedom of activity within the limits of his developmental stage of behavior restricts the use that may be made of the authority that the parent and teacher rightfully possess. This requires a high degree of resourcefulness and carefulness on the part of adults.

Both the child and the adult must possess an understanding of balanced values. Some commands should be obeyed promptly. Others should rest upon intelligent reflection and decision-making by the child. There should be gradual progress from obedience to directions given by those in authority to behavior responses based upon individual responsbility — from externally imposed discipline to individual self-discipline.

Role of Dominance. Domination plays an important role in training toward self-discipline. Behavior must be restricted, restrained, and controlled.

The behavior of an infant is more or less restricted by his parents. As the child matures, he needs a gradually increasing amount of freedom of choice or of decision-making. He is helped to become self-reliant if he is permitted some freedom in selecting the clothes he wears, the toy with he plays, or the child with whom he prefers to be.

It is normal for an adult to become emotionalized over a child's display of unco-operative behavior. Anger growing out of the situation experienced by the adult must be recognized and controlled by him, before he attempts to treat the child's misdemeanor. At the same time, the adult should understand the possible reasons for the child's display of anger in the same situation. Sometimes, the child is reacting in imitation of the adult.

Punishment. Punishment acts to deter undesirable individual behavior and to help establish group values of right and wrong. The extent to which techniques of punishment should be used for these purposes is an open question. It is believed by some psychologists that a child can achieve self-discipline more quickly if he is allowed to suffer the natural punishment that may accompany misbehavior. Mild natural punishments probably are desirable. If this theory of punishment is carried to an extreme, the consequences may be extremely harmful to the child. Punishment for the sake of punishment is likely to produce other but equally disastrous results.

The seriousness of his offense should be understood by the child. He usually evaluates the seriousness of his offense in terms of the kind of amount of punishment he receives. Hence, punishment should never be more severe than sufficient to meet the correction of the immediate behavior problem.

The child appreciates the attitude of the adult who evaluates childish behavior in terms of the factors that stimulate it. The child guilty of self-initiated misbehavior is less likely to resent just punishment than the child who feels that he is being punished for a misdemeanor, the engaging in which is not completely his fault.

Whatever form of punishment is utilized by the adult, certain procedures should be followed in its administration. Punishment should be consistent and administered promptly. The child should know why he is being punished. The punishment should not be harsh, cruel, or prolonged; neither should the child be reminded constantly of his former misdeeds and threatened with punishment if they reoccur. After the punishment has been administered, the incident should be closed and the child reassured of the adult's affection for him. Many misdemeanors and consequent punishment could be avoided if the adult consciously tried to take the child into his confidence, to assign tasks that are not too difficult for him, to display a sense of humor in his relations with him, and to display a positive rather than a negative attitude.

Reward. The concept of reward as a means of promoting personally and socially desirable behavior is inherent in the acceptance of motivation as a stimulating force in behavior direction. The child can be encouraged by the utilization of one or another incentive to engage in the kind of behavior which will earn for him the respect of his associates.

The value of reward in the form of constructive approval, praise, and the like has been considered variously in other sections of this book. At this point, emphasis is placed upon the psychological values to be achieved by attempts to utilize rewards in the formation of a child's behavior pattern.

There are times when it becomes necessary to make use of extrinsic rewards in order to stimulate continuation of desirable behavior, or to start desired behavior on the part of a misbehaving child or a child who has developed habit patterns that do not conform to present group living. Rewards are bad, however, if a great part of the child's life comes to revolve around them. The use of stars, special privileges, or even approval can be overdone. Unless rewards can be used in some way to build up pleasant associations with the desired behavior itself they had better not be introduced.

It is the custom in some homes for a child to receive payment for the performance of one or another home chore. Authorities disagree concerning the desirability of this practice. It would seem that paying a child to do something that is closely related to family welfare might exclude the child from the kind of unity that is characteristic of a closely knit, interco-operating family group, in which each member takes his share of responsibility for the family welfare. The situation is different, and the child probably deserves special recognition in the form of a reward, if he assumes responsibility for a chore that is the accustomed responsibility of another member of the family.

Intrinsic rewards that can be tied up closely with desired behavior, such as social recognition in the form of praise, can be used effectively. The granting of special privileges to an individual child, or to a group of children who have shown definite attempts at cooperation, is much appreciated by them and stimulates them to further desirable behavior.

Rigid Controls versus Democratic Discipline. Not all adults agree as to what constitutes socially accepted behavior. Some are unduly autocratic or rigid, others are extremely permissive. Hence the need for rules and regulations to protect the welfare of all. The child who is excused because of his immaturity, from following simple rules of conduct is likely to acquire behavior habits that show lack of consideration for others. A child who can be helped to so behave that he does not bring hurt either to himself or to others. This is a democratic approach to the achievement of self-control. This is a kind of two-way street that enables the child to be protected and to protect others.

Rigid, authoratarian discipline is the anthisis of the democratic approach. The adult sets standards of conduct and demands conformity to them by the child. Rules and regulations are established in the home and school that are to be obeyed regard-less of their resonableness. The effect on a child reared in a rigidly-controlled home and of a child reared in a democratic situation differs greatly. The child reared in a controlled environment tends to be quiet, nonresistant, well-behaved, and nonaggressive with restricted curiosity, originality or forcefulness. The child in the democratic atmosphere is likely to be an active, aggressive, fearless and playful individual.

The child reared under rigid controls either may become a submissive, self restrained adult or, when freed from parental domination, may make an about face and become domineering and demanding. Delinquent behavior during adolescence may well be an outgrowth of experiencing either extreme permissiveness or too rigid behavior control during childhood years.

Value of Democratic Discipline in Developing Self-control. In a democratic society, behavior controls need to be democratically evolved. Democratic discipline is effective and valuable to the child to the extent that it:

1. Promotes the development of self-discipline.
2. Develops his concept of self as a worthwile individual.
3. Enables him to know himself better as a unique person.
4. Utilizes the principles of freedom, justice, and equality of opportunity.

5. Encourages him to discover new ways in meeting his needs.
7. Makes use of judicial controls.
8. Increases his readiness for further self-direction.
9. Helps him to initiate proper action rather than behaving according to the dictates of others.
10. Performs in a basically consistent manner.
11. Utilizes intrinsic rewards.
12. Avoids the use of punishment as a planned deterrent.
13. Avoids the use of blame and recrimination.
14. Enables him to become self-reliant.

Self-discipline is developed by guiding the child through early child impulsiveness to more mature understanding of his social role. Through imitation the child comes to realize his need for social conformity. He achieves an understanding of what is expected from him through adult example and through play and other learning activities of his own age group.

The child needs many opportunities to develop self-control. He needs freedom within appropriate limits. Both boys and girls need help in finding ways in which to develop an attitude of accepting responsibilities, such as conforming to reasonable regulations, developing skill in group relationships, engaging in home chores and school study, and doing a little more than minimum requirements in assigned tasks.

CHAPTER 12

The development of Personality

Throughout his life an individual experiences many and various needs that must be satisfied to ensure survival. He gradually acquires more or less habitual ways of satisfying these needs. His expressed needs and his customary modes of satisfying these needs as observed by those around him are evaluated by his associates. To that extent they constitute his individual personality.

THE PERSONALITY PATTERN

As the child passes progressively through the various aspects of his growth and development from the prenatal period through adolescence to adulthood, a constant and more or less consistent integration or process of interrelationship is taking place among all his characteristics. *Personality* is the term generally used to describe the over-all behavior pattern at any stage of his development.

Meaning of Personality. Personality (a difficult term to define) can be thought of as including all the areas of development considered in earlier chapters: physical, motor, language, mental, emotional, social, and moral. Personality represents more than the sum total of these various components, however. It rather is a theoretical or abstract concept or generalization that connotes the qualitative nature of development. By this is meant the ways in which the various characteristics are interrelated and the degree to which they influence one another and the individual's total behavior pattern.

Personality grows out of a multitude of dynamic responses to many and different dynamic environmental influences. It is revealed through activity as a child's or older person's inner wants, urges, and impulses interact with persons or forces in his environment. For convenience of study, an individual's personality can be regarded as consisting of traits or individual behavior qualities. These do not function separately, however, but react with one another more or less consistently.

Approaches to the Study of Personality. Interest in personality has existed from ancient times onward. Attempted explanations of personality range from philosophic speculation to complex theoretical systems. Many attempts have been made to classify individuals according to type of personality. At present, the theory that the behavior of an individual places him in one or another category of personality is losing favor, since so many differences can be observed among individuals that no one person exhibits what might be called the characteristics of a "pure" type.

For example, one of the most popular classifications is based on Jung's attempt to explain personality differences in terms of introvert (ingoing) or extrovert (outgoing) characteristics. He listed certain traits that supposedly are associated with introversion and others that represent extroversion. It was found, however, that many persons display some behavior attributes that are introverted and others that are extroverted. Hence, a third category, ambiversion, had to be added to the other two as representing a combination of introvert and extrovert types. Consequently, for practical purposes, the classification broke down, except in cases of serious mental illness in which the patient may withdraw almost completely within himself, or become extremely loud and boisterous, or exhibit extreme, unrealistic concern with things and people about him.

The first attempts at what might be referred to as the *genetic approach* in the study of psychological characteristics began early in the twentieth century. Gesell's detailed biographical and clinical study of child development has resulted in a theory of personality based upon a descriptive analysis of the child's stages of development. He includes in his studies some interpretation of the behavior of the child at respective stages which can serve as predictive of what may be expected to be sequential in further development.

The Gestalt approach to the study of personality represents an attempt to discover the general laws of personality dynamics that underlie individual differences among children. As conceived by Murray, for example, personality represents an integration of the

162

individual's personal and social needs with what he calls a "perceptual press" or the effect upon an individual's well-being of the extent to which and the ways in which his needs are satisfied. A *thema* is interpreted as the behavior resolution of a particular need-press situation. Murray has developed the Thematic Apperception Test which will be discussed later in this chapter.

Shirley made a study of the early reactions of children and concluded that, although environment plays a large part in personality development, the major influence is heredity. Some psychologists claim that some personality traits are more flexible than others — they respond more easily and quickly to change.

THE GROWTH OF PERSONALITY

Because of the complexity of the personality pattern, it is difficult to trace its sequential development. Some psychologists claim that personality differences show themselves at birth. Others believe that personality, as they define it, cannot be observed as such until the child gives overt expression to a recognition of himself as an individual among other individuals. There are, however, differences in behavior that show themselves early and appear to maintain a certain amount of consistency through the developmental period.

Personality of the Very Young Child. Studies of newborn infants indicate that even during the earliest period there are differnces in child behavior. One child is placid and quiet; another is restless, cries, and gives evidence of irritability. Whether the child is a full-term or a premature baby as well as the conditions during his delivery may affect the general pattern of his behavior at birth.

Differences in behavior even among children of the same family have been observed during their neonatal period. The behavior and general constitution of the young child show differences in amount and kind of activity, muscle tone, degree of co-ordination, muscular energy, tolerance of physical discomfort, readiness to smile or to cry, and similar reactions. It is believed by some psychologists that in these early responses can be found the "nucleus of personality" that is the resultant of the neonate's degree of nervous plasticity, glandular functioning, and sex. According to some studies, the activity pattern of a child tends to persist, although it can be modified during the growing years by physical and psychological changes within and outside the child.

During the first two years, behavior habits may be formed that have a significant effect upon the child's developing personality. He may give evidence of a relatively definite behavior pattern by the time he has reached his third birthday. Consistency of behavior may not be evident in another child until he has reached school age. A relatively small number of children do not seem to achieve observable consistency of personality until adolescence or later. Many factors are responsible for variation in the acquisition of a mature personality. One that has been emphasized is the time at which and the degree to which a basic security in social relationships is achieved.

Personality of the Preschool Child. The preschool child develops some definite understanding of personal-social relationships. In the average home, the child is closely attached to his mother. He may or may not accept his father. If he believes that his father is getting some of the attention from the mother that should go to him, he may resent the father. The child may allow his father to care for some of his needs, especially if this parent has been accustomed to share the care of the child with the mother or if the mother is ill or absent.

The child's attitude toward his brothers and sisters differs in terms of their age in comparison to his. He may tease or quarrel with older siblings but usually is thoughtful and kindly in his relationships with younger members of the family. The child's attitudes toward the members of his family may be unpredictable, depending upon the extent to which his personal interests are interfered with by the others.

In his relationships with adults and children outside the home, the preschool child may exhibit better manners than he does in the intimacy of family life. He may form close attachments to adults, especially those who make a fuss over him, and he can be expected by the age of five to play well with other children.

In all these relationships, characteristic personality patterns are exhibited. Sex differences may be marked. The girl appears to exhibit a greater degree of emotionalized behavior than does the boy of the same age.

Personality during Elementary School Years. The elementary school child usually is a happy child. His developing personality traits can be molded within the limits of innate potentialities. He becomes more independent and self-reliant. His growing self-realization may cause him to vary in his attitudes toward his mother and father. He still needs the experience of security in their affection and care for him, but he may resent their apparently unjust curbing of his interests and activities. His attitude toward other siblings may show the same variation. He teases, but at the same time he is willing to take care of younger children and is prou'd of the accomplishments of his older brothers and sisters.

Outside the home, the child tends to be self-inhibiting, courteous, and generally friendly. He usually likes his teachers and strives to please them. He may become so attached to a particular teacher that he is willing to forgo promotion to the next grade in order to remain with his beloved teacher. This attitude may be caused by the fact that he has not yet achieved a feeling of complete security in his out-of-home relationships and is reluctant to face the new situation of finding security in another adult whose demands upon him he may think to be beyond his power to meet.

This is the period of the "best friend" relationship. A child's developing traits may be influenced significantly by the attitudes that develop during the series of child intimacies with another member of the same sex. As two young people discuss with each other their "secret" feelings and interests and share their activities, they are thereby developing a philosophy of life that may affect their present and future attitude and behavior.

As a rule, children of this age period get along acceptably in group relationships. They are drawn together by similarities of interests and are eager to exhibit to one another their particular abilities in work or play activity. Disagreements and quarrels may, of course, interfere with the maintenance of satisfying group relationships. Some of these disagreements arise in the desire of one or another member to assert his personality through aggressive behavior.

Results of studies dealing with the development of personality traits indicate that some children evidence a persistency of traits that are exhibited early. In most cases, even the persistent traits undergo modification of one sort or another during the developing years. A child tends to live up to adult evaluation of himself, as quick or slow, good or bad, lazy or helpful, and the like.

Personality through Early Adolescence. The physical changes that take place during adolescence may have a powerful effect upon a young person's personality pattern. What may seem to some adults to be radical personality changes are brought about by new attitudes to be radical personality changes are brought about by new attitudes toward himself and his relationships with others, especially members of the opposite sex, new interests growing out of pubertal changes, and the impact upon his personality of the enlarged environments of junior and senior high school. Fundamental attitudes and behavior patterns continue to exist but take on different meaning and form.

Ideals change from those exhibited by the average child under twelve years of age. Studies of the personality traits of their peers admired by the twelve- to fifteen-year-old indicate that traits admired formerly now are regarded as babyish.

At twelve, the girl admires and attempts to emulate a personality pattern that is in accordance with adult ideals. By the time she reaches the age of fifteen she apparently is less concerned with adult standards. She strives to be an outgoing, glamorous person. She is active in many ways, and may be a successful leader of parties and games and a good sport, in terms of adolescent ideals.

A boy shows leadership changes during these years. The twelve-yera-old tends to be an individualist, defying adult-made regulations. He may be fearless, daring, active and skillful in sports, and a leader in boys' games and other activities. As he approaches the middle adolescent years, the boy wants to exhibit "manly" characteristics, including a mature acceptance of adult standards of behavior.

A young person of either sex may be unable to meet successfully the standards of what to him constitute desirable personality characteristics. His failure may result in more or less serious delinquent behavior or emotional disturbances.

FACTORS THAT INFLUENCE PERSONALITY DEVELOPMENT

It probably is impossible to categorize and treat separately the many variables that influence a child's personality. The acceptance of the concept of integration as applied to personality development must be accompanied by a recognition of the fact that an individual is building his personality pattern through constant interaction within himself and with the outer environmental influences to which he is exposed. His potentialities and limitations determine the ways in which and the extent to which any one or more of his environmental experiences will affect him. Also, various combinations of inner reactions and outer influences will result in varying forms of integration.

Any isolated consideration of the factors that influence the development of the various personality traits can be one of convenience only. The treatment of any one of them separately must take into account its proper and differing relationships to all the others.

Factors Inherent in the Individual's Constitution. The child's physical structure, physiological status, and motor, mental, and emotional potentialities affect his attitudes and behavior. His personality pattern at any stage of development is influenced by the various aspects of his general constitution. As an individual he affects others. This effect is reflected in his reactions as he becomes aware of the opinions of his associates concerning him.

Body Structure and Physical Condition. In his relation to his peers, a strong, healthy child has an advantage over smaller and more fragile children. He is able to participate in activities suitable to his stage of development.

The exceptionally tall or short child, or the excessively thin or stout child, is regarded as a deviate by other, more normal children. He may become the victim of unkind teasing or name-calling. The small, physically underdeveloped child may acquire feelings of inferiority if he is rejected by his age group and not permitted to participate in their accustomed activities.

The child's physical status may affect parental attitudes toward him. The physically well-developed child is expected to behave in a more mature manner than his total developmental pattern warrants. The small, delicate child may be overprotected by an anxious, zealous mother. She denies him the freedom of action granted to a larger size and constitution, his mother may not be able to forget his early smallness and fragility. She continues to coddle him and to restrict his activities.

Size and color of eyes, color and curliness of hair, and texture and condition of skin also affect a growing child's attitudes toward himself. Undue emphasis by adults on his appearance may give rise to an exaggerated opinion of his attractiveness if their comments are favorable. Self-pity or self-abnegation may result if the comments are derogatory. Some of these attitudes developed during childhood may persist long after there is any valid reason for their being experienced.

Physical handicaps, such as a crippled or deformed body,

blindness or near-blindness, hearing difficulties, a delicate constitution, and susceptibility to allergies usually have an unfavorable effect upon the child's disposition. He may exhibit one or more undesirable modes of behavior: irritability, overaggression, timidity, or emotional instability. The extent to which the afflicted child displays any of these characteristics depends in good part upon the attitudes exhibited by his associates toward him and his physical affliction.

Motor Co-ordination. A child enjoys engaging in activities that involve muscular strength and motor co-ordination. He wants to excel in such activities. He earns the admiration and respect of his peers if he equals or excels them in performance. If he exhibits too great superiority he may be resented by his own age group. He is impelled thereby to compete with children older than himself who may not be tolerant of his other, less mature characteristics. This nonacceptance by either group may encourage him to bully younger children who do not dare reject him completely for fear of what he might do to them if they did.

The child who is below average in muscular strength and motor co-ordination is fearful, timid, and perhaps frustrated. This is especially true if oversolicitous parents are unwilling for him to participate in what would be normal activities for his age status. These parents fear that he might hurt himself.

General Mental Ability and Special Aptitudes. The mentally alert individual can adjust to environmental conditions and social standards more easily than can the slow responder. The bright child is able earlier than others to recognize the relationship of himself to persons and things in his environment. To the extent that during his early years he has been encouraged to want to make desirable adjustments, he is quick to understand what these should be in terms of his stage of maturity and the demands made upon him.

Superior Intelligence. The exceptionally bright child experiences adjustment difficulties that are the outgrowth of his mental superiority. Overpraise of his early precocious behavior may cause him to develop an overappreciation of himself and his abilities. Because of his relatively mature understanding he may be bored as well as resented by other members of his own age group. He is still too immature in other ways to be accepted by older children. Hence, he may become a lonely isolate who finds his chief avenue of satisfaction that of excelling his classmates in book knowledge. Since the mentally superior child may not possess an

168

equal superiority in mechanical skills, he is hesitant to meet competition in them and may be unwilling to develop any little mechanical ability that he possesses unless he is guided carefully.

The mentally superior child, especially during the later years of childhood and of early adolescence, often is able to recognize the inconsistency and irrationalism of adult regulations and dictums. Consequently, he may resent or assume a negative attitude toward any adult authority. If older adults, however, recognize the child's relatively mature pattern of thought and treat him accordingly, he will seek their company and withdraw even more from association with younger people. Teachers often have difficulty with their bright pupils who want to monopolize an undue amount of the teacher's time, both during and after regular school hours.

Mental Retardation. The slow child experiences problems of personality adjustment that are different from those of the bright child but equally serious. Parents seem to be unwilling to admit that their child may be unable to compete with more alert children. They tend to force him beyond his mental limits and show impatience if he cannot meet their expectations. When or if they recognize his inadequacies, they may attempt to excuse his slowness by asserting that he still is only a baby, thus protecting him from unfavorable criticisms by others.

When the slow child is forced in school to compete with children brighter than himself, he experiences failure and recognizes his own lack of ability. The fact that other children may call him "dumb" and exclude him from their group activities intensifies his feelings of inadequacy. Home attitudes combined with those experienced in school may cause him to develop a personality pattern that exhibits definite feelings of inferiority.

The situation of the slow child is not helped any if, in his immature way, he attempts to buy his way into the good graces of his associates. He soon comes to realize that the others like what they get from him without any change in their attitude toward him as a person. This kind of experience may intensify personal bitterness and antisocial attitudes, which in adulthood may be extended to include society as a whole.

Special Aptitude. A child may exhibit the possession of marked ability or of superior aptitude in a special field, such as music, art, writing, or acting. This aptitude helps him to find a place for himself among his fellows if his superiority to them in this respect is not too great. The gifted person who can and will use his talent for the benefit or entertainment of the group is a welcome addition to that group. The admiration and appreciation he receives cause him to feel friendly toward others and to be expansive in his relationships with them.

If the young person's aptitude in any field is markedly superior to that of the other members of his group, he may have experiences and develop attitudes similar to those of the mentally very superior. Also, his special aptitude may be given too great attention by the family, and he may come to consider himself in a class by himself. If training leads to exceptional performance he is likely to come into the limelight of attention. He may retreat from public adulation and become shy and retiring. Usually the opposite attitude develops. He seeks attention. When he receives it, he may become selfish, self-centered, and aggressive.

The Emotions. During his early years a child may appear to be relatively apathetic or phlegmatic, or he may exhibit highly excited behavior. The child's emotional reactions are tied up with his other developing patterns of behavior. An individual's interreactions with his environment are affected by his temperamental self. What may be disregarded as nonimportant by one child may be a matter of great moment to another. Training and experience have some bearing upon a child's emotionalized attitudes, but there seem to be differences that are inherent and that are closely linked with the functioning of the glandular and autonomic nervous systems.

As the child progresses through his maturing years, he develops behavior patterns that cause him to impress people variously as cheerful, quick-tempered, kindly, sympathetic, patient, understanding, co-operative, irritable, affectionate, cruel, friendly, grouchy, and the like. Regardless of the extent to which these impressions have validity in fact or of how a specific characteristic has been acquired, the effect that the child or older individual has upon other people influences to a great extent the subsequent attitudes and forms of behavior that constitute his personality pattern.

Environmental Factors of Influence. As has been said earlier, all the conditions and persons that constitute a child's environment have a tremendous influence upon his developing personality. Among the most significant of these are the home, the school, peer associates, and other factors that may be more or less incidental.

The Home. The influence of home conditions and family attitudes and behavior have been discussed previously. At this point, attention is directed to some of the most significant aspects of home life in personality development.

Some of the characteristics of the home that afford opportunities to a child to develop socially acceptable personality traits are the following:

1. Willingness on the part of adults to accept the child as a worthy member of the family.

2. A minimum of disagreement and discord, especially in the presence of a child.

3. A democratic attitude which permits each member of the family to follow his own interests insofar as these do not interfere with the welfare of others in or outside the family group.

4. Good adjustment of father and mother to the marital state.

5. Adequate, though not necessarily superior, economic status.

6. Social acceptance of the family by neighbors.

The attitudes and behavior patterns of the members of the family group that are unfavorble to the child's achievement of good personality adjustment would be the reverse of those listed in the foregoing. A child is hindered rather than helped in his struggle for acceptance by a larger social group if he is reared in a home in which there is little or no family co-operation, in which high standards of personal behavior are not evident, in which the child is not expected to acquire socially acceptable behavior habits, or in which the parents patently are mismated and make no effort to conceal this fact from the child.

There is doubt among psychologists concerning the importance to the child of the economic status of his family. The actual size of the family budget does not seem to be too significant a factor, if the home is simple but clean and neat, if the child receives sufficient and healthful food, and if the attitudes of the family members are such that he can experience feelings of security.

The School. Many investigations have been made concerning the part played by the school in the development of a child's personality. These include three areas of study: the curriculum and the child, teacher-pupil relations, and child-child relations.

The Curriculum and the Child. Much attention is being given at present to what the child should learn in school and how he should learn it. Many psychologists and educators believe that the formalized curriculums and more or less rigid disciplines of the so-called traditional school exerted a very unfavorable effect upon the

171

child's developing personality. Hence, some psychologists have recommended certain changes, and educators have attempted to put them into practice. A few of the most significant of these recommendations are:

1. The curriculum should be adjusted to the child's developmental learning status.

2. The content of the curriculum should include those skills, knowledges, and attitudes which the child can utilize in his present experiences as well as those which fit him for his future educational needs.

3. The child should be encouraged to learn through his own activity rather than be a passive recipient of teacher activity.

4. To as great an extent as possible, the child's learning should follow the interests and desires that are the concomitants of his present stage of development, rather than be dictated by adult belief as to what his learning interests should be.

Teacher-Pupil Relations. A teacher exercises considerable influence upon the child's development of attitudes, standards, and ideals of behavior. During the elementary school period the child tends to regard the teacher as the source of all wisdom, and to imitate teacher behavior. The child also is sensitive to behavior traits exhibited by the teacher, such as degree of fairness and justice, honesty, appreciation of effort, sympathy and understanding, ability to explain things, and expectation of cooperative and controlled behavior on the part of the child. The particular attitude displayed by the teacher toward the child affects the latter significantly.

Teacher-pupil relations during the adolescent years may not be so personal as they were during childhood. The teacher's influence upon the maturing young person, however, may be even greater in some ways than it was earlier. The admired teacher of the same sex becomes the model which the adolescent strives to imitate.

Child-Child Relationships. In school as well as out a child's personality is much influenced by the personality traits of his peers. In the school situation he learns to work with others as well as to play with them. As the child or young adolescent strives to find self-realization through accomplishment, he must compete with his own record as well as with the performance of others. The techniques of meeting competition that he finds to be successful in his relations with his schoolmates probably will become habitual to the extent that he is likely to employ them in his later business and social life. Hence, they will become an integral phase of his personality.

Other Factors of Influence. Each culture gives evidence of following certain approved patterns of behavior. These are important molders of the child's personality. Accepted ideals have to do with what is expected of an individual in such traits as trustworthiness, industry, co-operation, honesty, loyalty, and attitudes toward sex relations. The relative behavior attributes of boys and girls also have their cultural bases.

A child's practiced interests and hobbies affect his personality, and at the same time they are an outgrowth of his personality. A child who is afforded opportunities to engage in hobbies, whether these be long- or short-lived, usually is a more extroverted or outgoing individual than is the child who has few hobbies. Interests or hobbies that are shared with other children have a better total effect upon a child's personality than the hobbies of the lonely child who engages in such activities by himself as a substitute for companionship with his peers, which for one or another reason he is denied.

Another influence upon a child's personality is his name — his first name or the combination of his first and second name. To have the same first name as the parent may cause embarrassment to the child, especially if he is commonly referred to as "Junior" or as "little —." The appellation may endure beyond the age when it is appropriate.

The child may be made to feel uncomfortable if his name cannot be pronounced correctly by his playmates. He also may be disturbed if it lends itself to an abbreviated form, if it is considered too stylish or "sissy," or if it can be distorted or made the subject of jest, especially in combination with his surname. Certain nicknames that are accepted during childhood are deeply resented later. In certain neighborhoods, a child may experience deep humiliation and perhaps bitterness if his surname indicates that he is a member of a minority group in that particular neighborhood.

PERSONALITY EVALUATION

Various types of evaluating instruments have been devised to ascertain progress in the personality development of the child. Attempts are made to compare his stage of development with that of children of the same age and to discover whether he is suffering

173

from one or another form of personality maladjustment. The results obtained from the administration of these instruments are not completely satisfactory, since personality represents a complex structure that does not lend itself readily to evaluation.

The rating scales and other devices utilized vary in their functions. Some have been constructed in terms of the belief that personality represents the aggregate of separate traits or areas of response. Measurement and evaluation then are attempted by means of rating scales, questionnaires, and similar devices.

Other evaluating techniques are based upon the concept of personality as an integrated whole. The purpose of evaluation then becomes that of attempting to gain an understanding of the child's complex of inner attitude reactions. Materials used include situations in which the child may express his feelings and attitudes freely or project himself through such media as finger painting and easel painting, symbolic play, and responses to ink blots and pictures.

Rating by Others. Rating scales are used to discover what other people, who supposedly know the child well, think about his various personality traits in relation to the traits of others. A scale of this type is a measure of reputation. In its simplest form, the scale consists of *Yes* or *No* answers to questions such as "Is he generally cheerful?" or "Does he get along well with other children?"

Most scales allow for the evaluation of the child in terms of the degree to which he may possess a particular trait. In this form of scale, called the *graphic rating scale,* the rater indicates by an appropriate check where on the scale he believes the child belongs. He rates the child in relation to numerical value, usually from 5 to 1, each of which represents a descriptive term such as very superior (5), superior (4), average (3), inferior (2), very inferior (1). For example:

Is he socially adaptable?

Usually at ease in groups (4)	Awkward and ill at ease (2)	Completely at ease (5)	Unable to adjust to groups (1)	Able to adjust to groups if interested (3)

A "guess who" method of rating was devised by Hartshorne and May to obtain the judgment of children concerning the personality traits of their same-age associates. Word pictures that include descriptions of such characteristics as neatness or popularity are presented to the group. The children write down the name of the child or the names of the children who in their opinion fit particular word pictures. For example, "This one is always picking on others and annoying them."

Rating scales yield evaluations that are subjectively arrived at. The general attitude of the rater toward the subject is likely to color the rating of a particular trait. This "halo" effect may invalidate the rating. A more accurate appraisal is made possible by having the child rated by two or more individuals and combining the results.

Self-Appraisal Questionnaires. Many questionnaires have been devised to obtain from the child who can read and understand what he reads an evaluation of himself by himself in various personality areas. The answers usually are given in the form of *Yes, No,* and *?* *(Not sure)* to questions such as "Does your mother always treat you right?" or "Are you usually happy?"

One of the faults of self-evaluating questionnaires is that the child may answer as he thinks he should rather than as he really feels. The brighter the child, the more likely he is to attempt to give what to him appear acceptable answers.

Projective Techniques. These techniques are utilized with the child whose personality is to be evaluated. Particular traits are not isolated, but the child is encouraged to express in words or actions his inmost thoughts and attitudes as he responds freely in one way or another to the materials or evaluation. The administrator of the technique than attempts to evaluate the child's personality pattern, with special reference to maladjusting factors that are evidenced in the child's performance. This requires that the interpreter be well trained. Interpretations are difficult since there can be no specific norms. For this reason, much more experimentation with projective techniques is needed before they can be expected to yield completely valid results.

Finger Painting. The child is supposed to give expression to his emotionalized attitudes as he projects himself in more or less meaningful representations produced by painting with his fingers. The beginnings of creative ability can be discovered through the use of this technique. It also may have value as a therapeutic measure.

Easel Painting. This technique is used especially with preschool and early elementary school children. Through the medium of crayon or of water-color paints, the child expresses on large sheets of paper whatever he wishes. Younger children usually combine various colors in a smudged mass. Later, these unstructured forms gradually are superseded by attempts to represent objects in the child's environment.

The symbolism of the child's use of form, line, color, and space constitutes the basis of the analysis of his inner life. Therapists appear to consider the use of color the best indication of a child's emotional expression. The utilization of this technique for therapeutic purposes requires considerable skill. Its results should be combined with the results of other methods of studying the development of the child's personality.

Play Activities. In a well-equipped playroom, the child is permitted to play at will, unhampered by adult direction or suggestion. The materials in the room include a doll family and other things common to the average home with which the child can be expected to have had experience. The child's behavior is watched by the therapist (preferably through a one-way screen) and observations are made concerning the child's reactions to the various materials with which he plays.

It is believed that, as the child plays without restrictions, he is likely to give expression to his inner feelings toward the members of his family (symbolized by the dolls) and toward family activities. This technique must be used intelligently. Generalizations should be avoided concerning deep-seated emotional difficulties if they are based upon a few instances of what may seem to be maladjusted attitudes or behavior.

The Rorschach Test. The technique originated by Rorschach can be used with children, although it was devised primarily for use with adults. The subject is asked to interpret each of ten ink blots, some of which are colored. These have been standardized so that each of many various interpretations or combinations of interpretations has a specific connotation. There is a difference of opinion among psychologists concerning the validity of this technique. Even the highly trained therapist can make errors of judgment because of the subjective aspects of interpretation.

Thematic Apperception Tests. On each of two different days the subject is shown a set of ten pictures, in sequence. As he looks at each picture, the subject is asked to tell a story that is suggested to him by what he sees in the picture. By so doing, the individual is supposed to give oral expression to his pattern of thinking and to "the dominant drives, emotions, complexes and conflicts" of his personality.

Although this test was devised for use with adolescents, it has yielded relatively successful results with children of the age of seven years or older. The material includes nineteen pictures and one blank card. The methods of scoring and interpretation are standardized but contain subjective elements. Hence, as is found in other projective techniques, errors of judgment are possible.

Other pictorial techniques such as the *Children's Apperception Test* (CAT) and the Symonds *Picture Story Test for Adolescents,* are being used in school and private practice. As a subject is motivated to tell story after story concerning the respective pictures, certain attitudes continue to show themselves throughout the administration of the test.

Picture Frustration Technique. Rosenzweig devised a test to measure emotionalized attitudes. He undertook to measure three types of frustration: extrapunitive, intropunitive and impunitive. The test consists of a series of comic-strip-type pictures. Each sketch depicts a possible frustrating situation to which the subject responds by entering his actual expression in the space provided. He is invited to write "the first reply which comes to mind," and to "avoid being humorous." In general, the test helps to determine whether the subject attacks his environment, blames himself, or quietly ignores the problem.

Puppetry. Children respond in interesting ways to the action of puppets. Each child tends to identify himself with the puppet characters and the actions that are being portrayed by them. Each child tends to project his personal feelings, desires, and hopes into the puppet show.

Puppets are classified according to the method used to manipulate them: *shadow puppet, string puppet,* and *glove* or *hand puppet.* The shadow puppet is held close behind a translucent screen in such manner that a shadow is thrown on the screen. The viewer then sees the shadow and not the puppet. The string puppet (marionette) is a doll so joined that the head, arms, and legs can be moved by a human operator. The glove or hand puppet utilizes the anatomy of the hand to provide a three-dimensional head with a garb attached to it, and is manipulated by the hand of the performer.

The limited use that has been made of puppetry suggests that it can serve a valuable purpose in the understanding of some of the maladjustments of childhood. It shows promise of becoming a valuable therapeutic technique to be used in the study and analysis of deviating childhood behavior.

CHAPTER 13

Sexuality in Childhood

Some cultures of the recent past regarded the child as sexually innocent until glandular changes, marking the beginning of adolescence, resulted in the display in overt behavior of the developing sex urge. Psychoanalysts and clinicians, however, have presented evidence that sexuality may begin in infancy and continue to progress through differing stages during childhood and adolescence.

DEVELOPMENT OF SEXUAL INTERESTS

It cannot be denied that the sex drive plays an important role in the life of an individual. Yet the demands of a culture determine to some extent the nature of the child's developing pattern of sex interest. In some more primitive cultures the child, following the example of his elders, displays his sex interests freely. In our more rigid society the child's natural impulses are sometimes inhibited with the result that he may experience thwarting and frustration.

Modesty is often emphasized in the home. Before the child is old enough to recognize the reasons for his parents' attitudes, he may find that certain natural tendencies, such as viewing his parents when they are undressed, or a little boy's and a little girl's going to the bathroom together are not approved. These denials of his freedom may cause him to wonder about the denials. He may develop anxieties or guilt feelings about such matters, especially if he has attempted to engage in any sex-stimulated behavior which is unacceptable to his parents. The child's playing with his genitals is a case in point.

Influence of the Parent. The role played by each parent also can

179

affect a child's attitude toward sexual matters. If the father is the authority figure, and the mother is submissive to male domination, the child is likely to identify himself or herself with the female parent and share her fear of the male. It has been found that some adults have had difficulty in achieving good marital status because of the effect upon them of the relationship that existed between their parents, and of parents with themselves.

Age Differences in Sex Matters. The child's concern with sex changes with age. For example, the five-year-old child manifests an interest in reproduction and exhibitionism. He may indulge in sex play. The seven-year-old dreams about changing sex, and the eight-year-old, especially a girl, may ask how a baby comes. By the ages of nine and ten there is awareness of sexual differences and a curiosity about the genitals of his own sex. The ten-year-old girls are concerned about breast development. At age eleven, girls show definite adolescent reactions, and boys have frequent erections, tend to masturbate (although girls also may engage in this activity), and are curious about the sex life of animals. By the age of twelve, herteroxesual interests are present and concern with sexual matters becomes more realistic. By the fourteenth year at least half of the boys have ejaculations. Girls have individual friends, but boys tend to engage in gang activities. Anaxieties may arise concerning the body, and there may be some sexual activity. Boys tend to continue gang activities through their fifteenth year. There is group activity and little pairing off between the sexes but they engage in group activities that includes members of both sexes. By the time the young people have reached their sixteenth year, girls have come to accept their sexual role and boys, who find it difficult to control their sexual interests, tend to experiment. At present, this is true of girls also.

As sexual maturity approaches, the increased amounts of male and female sex hormones liberated in the blood stream stimulate the growth and development of accessary sex organs and result in the appearance of secondary sex characteristics. The changes that begin to appear at puberty include alterations in body contours, voice changes in boys, and breast development in girls. These changes are likely to be accompanied by differing emotional reactions among boys and girls.

The attitudes of growing boys and girls toward the physical and physiological changes that are taking place are much influenced by cultural mores in matters dealing with sexual maturation. In some sophisticated societal groups or subgroups these changes are played down. In our society sexual urges and interests are supposed to be sublimated until the individual is financially and socially fitted to choose a mate and accept adult responsibilities of marriage and the raising of a family. In more primitive or simple cultures the maturation of sex characteristics is considered to represent the onset of adulthood and the assumption of adult responsibilities for which the individual was prepared during his later childhood years.

PSYCHOANALYTIC THEORY OF SEXUALITY

According to psychoanalysts, there is continuous association between the sexual nature of the child and adult sexuality. Sexuality can be considered to be the fundamental motive of behavior. The sexual life of the individual is viewed, moreover, as including all behavior; it is not viewed in the narrow sense as referring only to sex-stimulated activity, as in the sex act.

The sexual energy of the individual from birth on, which can give him pleasure, is regarded as the *libido*. This energy is general in that pleasure can be gained from any act, but its expression is specifically sexual. Freud held that the roots of sexuality are in specific biological drives, but that sexual behavior is displayed generally in tendencies to experience emotional involvement in people or things. When these impulses are not accepted by society, they can be sublimated in such ways that they will be socially desirable.

According to the psychanalytic theory, the child passes through the following periods of sexual development: *oral, anal, phallic, latent* and *genital.* During early infancy the child derives libidinal satisfaction from oral activity and sucking. During the second year the libido expresses itself through anal activities, which finally give way to genital libidinal satisfactions. I now shall consider each of the stages of sexual development, including some of the problems and anxieties of the various stages as the self-concept matures from the satisfaction of *id* impulses through *ego* and *superego* controls. It must be remembered that although each stage is treated separately, there may be much overlapping among the stages.

The Oral Stage. The stimulation of any of the highly sensitive erogenous zones of the body results in what can be called erotic pleasure. The first of these zones includes the lips, tongue, mouth and cheeks. The child enjoys sucking his mother's breast, his thumb, or other object. The fact that during the first year of his life every small thing that he can reach finds its way into his mouth indicates the pleasure to his libido of stimulating these erogenous zones.

Oral activity at first is relatively passive. The young infant sucks anything that comes to his mouth, but he does not seek objects to place there. This phase of oral activity is important to psychoanalysts, as it represents a tendency of the individual in later life to meet the problem of accepting gratuities patiently, being dependent on others for one's welfare, and trusting others. The more active oral period begins with the eruption of the first teeth. The pain of their eruption causes the baby to bite, thereby causing suffering to the mother and interfering with her attempts at weaning. This is known as the oral-sadistic period.

Young children differ in their ability to accept an early deprivation of sucking or biting. For example, if five- or six-year-old is jealous of a new baby in the family, he may regress to this form of infant behavior. In fact, it is possible to find an individual of any age who finds it difficult to adjust to any form of deprivation. He may be motivated to respond to frustrating experiences by taking what he wants without consideration of the rights of another person or by hostile attacks.

The Anal Stage. The oral stage usually has ended by the beginning of the second year. The anal stage, as a period of libidinal satisfaction, continues from about the age of eighteen months to about three years. In our culture it is associated with toilet training. The child derives pleasure from excretion. He also senses the mother's attitude toward his bowel movements. She is pleased when he excretes, bothered when he does not.

The time at which an attitude of disgust toward his excretion begins depends on adult stimulation. Cleanliness, neatness and punctuality are learned responses. The child receives an understanding of what they mean by imitation of adult example. Moreover, the child who does not take readily to toilet training may suffer frustrations in his relationship with his mother. He may display his hostility by expulsion at the wrong time or by refusing to defecate when he is supposed to do so. This period is sometimes referred to as the anal-sadistic stage because of the elements of expulsion and destruction associated with it and the hostility engendered by the mother's insistence upon the child's following her will in matters of defecation and urination.

182

The Phallic Stage. From about the third to the sixth year the child passes through the phallic or early genital stage during which the genital zone becomes the center of libidinal satisfaction. Although fingering of the genitals and body exploration may have occurred earlier, this form of pleasure is intensified at this age period, with the boy in the penis, and the girl in the clitoris.

Freud believed that the *Oedipus complex* develops in the boy and the *Electra complex* in the girl. To this time, the mother has been the love object of the child. As the boy grows more aware of the fact that the father is given privileges by the mother which are denied him, he becomes jealous of his father as a rival. In fact, he is hostile to all of society. Gradually, the boy loses his great involvement with his mother but may continue to be hostile to his father. Eventually, a feeling of tenderness is likely to develop toward both parents.

The shift in loyalty from the mother to the father may be more difficult for the girl than it is for the boy. The latter began with his love for his mother, which is intensified. The girl's first object of love was the mother. She becomes aware of the differences in the genital organs of the male and the female. She recognizes the fact that she has no penis and wants to have one. Since she also may have developed feelings of hostility toward her mother as a result of weaning and toilet training, the satisfaction of libidinal energy is achieved through shifting her love to her father — the *Electra Complex.* She identifies with the mother as a rival for the father's affection.

The Latency Stage. Between the ages of about six to puberty, no new libidinal pleasure areas are experienced. This is referred to as the latency period, although this does not imply that there are no sexual satisfactions during these years. Masturbation and body play occur. Sexual interests may be less evident, however. Involvement with parents now takes the form of respect and affection.

The child becomes engrossed in many activities and wants to do things with individuals outside the home, especially with members of peer-age and same-sex groups and other interesting persons whom he meets in the school and community. As his environmental horizons broaden, he becomes curious, and his behavior is governed increasingly by the direction of his superego or conscience. He tends not to suffer from anxieties and feelings of guilt.

The Later Genital Stage. The later genital stage begins in the prepubertal period, starting at the age of about ten, and is intensified during the pubertal period. The prepubertal period may be marked by a return to earlier stages of libidinal satisfaction. Oedipal desires show themselves in the form of daydreams and fantasies in which castration and penis envy play their part. The personality of the child appears to change. Aggressive behavior may be displayed; anxieties concerned with the self are experienced.

During the prepubertal period, habits of cleanliness may be disregarded or become intensified. The young person may arise early, take cold showers, or lose interest in the companionship of his peers. Contrariwise, the child may engage with members of his peer group in philosophical discussions of religion, love and marriage, and life in general, although his concepts are immature.

A girl of this age may attempt to attract the attention of older boys, since same-age boys are likely to show their growing sex interest by a superficial lack of interest in the other sex. The child may develop a "crush" on an older member of the same or opposite sex. These involvements usually are short lived, however. During this period the young male seems to dislike any overt expression of parental affection toward him. He becomes extremely objective in his relationships with them. In his attitudes toward his parents and toward members of both sexes outside the home, he is beginning to give evidence of his gradual unconscious preparation for later heterosexual activities.

EDUCATION FOR SEXUAL UNDERSTANDING

The term *sex education* has come into question because it is often interpreted as meaning only the giving of information about sex acts and the physical structure and function of the sex organs. Education for sexual understanding includes both physical structure and physiological function, and the development of wholesome attitudes toward one's own body and toward members of both sexes.

Attitudes toward Sex Education. Many parents and educators of the past viewed with distrust any attempts to prepare a child for his sexual life. It was presumed that in one or another fashion he gradually would learn all that he needed to know. The results were that (1) some children accumulated much misinformation from older boys and girls who themselves were misinformed or had acquired abnormal attitudes toward sex, or (2) some young adults entered into the marital state impulsively with little or no comprehension of their role as mate or parent.

There is a growing agreement among parents, teachers, and community leaders that children need preparation for participation in the sex-motivated aspects of life. The question arises as to who should offer this education. The author believes that it should begin in the home and that much of it should be continued there. Religious leaders also can share this responsibility. The school also should make a contribution by introducing courses in sex education and employing well qualified teachers to teach them.

In the classroom, boys and girls can be motivated by an emotionally well-adjusted teacher to develop attitudes of respect and friendliness toward members of the opposite sex. In biology classes physical structure and physiological function can be presented. Health education can stress healthful living. Literature is replete with excellent examples of good home relationships which can be brought to the attention of young people. In addition, an individual child can discuss his own difficulties in private with his teacher or with a wise counselor.

Regardless of who offers the instruction, it needs to be presented objectively and unemotionally. Much of it, especially attitude development, can be indirect and permeate all the relationships with the child. Perhaps the attitude aspect is even more important than the mastery of factual material. The program of education can be well organized and presented gradually when the child is ready for it, step by step. A frank, honest approach, with no undue emphasis, does not shock young children, make them unduly curious, or lead to experimentation and socially unacceptable behavior. The children can accept this information in stride as they accept what they learn in other areas of knowledge.

Specific Suggestions. Education to help the child gain an under-standing of sex can begin in babyhood. The correct names of all parts of the body, including the so-called "privates," should be given whenever there is any occasion to use the terms. As soon as the child begins to ask questions, these should be answered briefly but correctly. For example, if the preschool child asks where babies come from, it may be sufficient to answer, "from inside the mother's body." Children usually are satisfied with short but what, to them, seem to be honest answers.

If the child persists by asking further, "How does the baby get there?'' the parent can answer simply, "The father places a little seed in her body which then starts to grow and comes out as a baby.'' 'It is not intended here to present suggested answers to all of children's questions. Various adults answer children's questions differently. I wish to emphasize the fact that the parent or other adult should not engage in long explanations, much of which may be beyond the child's comprehension. Children who help their parents in the garden or who are encouraged to have pets can learn much from their experiences, especially if the parents encourage questions and answer them appropriately.

Sometimes parents believe that the best approach with a child who has learned to read is to supply him or her with one of the simple books on the subject which now are available. Getting information from a book is better than receiving no information or getting misinformation, but better attitudes are developed if parent and child together read and discuss the material. Children tend to bring their first questions to the mother. This is to be expected as the mother, at least in the early years, is the chosen confidante of the child. Gradually, however, both father and mother can participate in this activity, preferably together.

As children approach adolescence it may be well for the mother to prepare her daughter for her first menstruation, and the father for his son's first ejaculation. Some parents tend to delay this preparation until the child experiences the first manifestation of changed physical status. Preparation, enough in advance to avoid anxiety-stimulating situations, has been found to be helpful to the maturing young person. It also has been the experience of adults who have given time, effort, and perhaps prayerful consideration to the sex education of their child, that as the young person meets problems of sexual adjustment during the adolescent years, the boy or girl will bring these problems to the adult for help in their solution.

CHAPTER 14

Adjustment During Childhood

At one time, temper tantrums, truancy, and other forms of delinquent behavior were considered to be manifestations of a child's selfishness, obstinacy, or meanness. Such behavior no longer is regarded as an outward manifestation of "bad" inner drives. It now is believed that a child's motives are essentially good and that disapproved behavior is learned in the same way as approved behavior. All behavior is the resultant of the effect of environmental influences upon inherent potentialities.

DEVIATE BEHAVIOR AND ITS CAUSES

From the mental hygiene point of view, deviate behavior is characterized as eccentric, neurotic, or psychotic. A variety of conditions or situations may account for deviate behavior. Instead of holding a maladjusted child or adult accountable for his unfortunate condition, an effort is being made to discover the underlying causes of the difficulty, whether these lie within or outside the individual.

Types of Causes. Physiological disorders undoubtedly account for their share of behavior abnormalities. The cause, however, is as likely to be found in the immediate environment, such as mental deficiency or moral delinquency of parent or parents, a broken home, lack of parental attention or care, or other maladjustive factors. The present spread of emotional disturbance and mental illness has been caused both by the complexity of modern civilization and by ignorance among laymen, teachers, and other adults concerning the factors that act as predispositions to mental breakdown and emotional disturbances.

Abnormal behavior is generally recognized to be caused by (1) predisposing factors and (2) exciting factors. Some of the predispositions are inherited and some develop through conditioning, such as drugs, physical illness, shock, or disease. Mental maladjustments in children usually are accompanied by emotional difficulties. No general formula can be suggested for the treatment of maladjusted children, since the causes differ and probably are not alike for any two.

Unfavorable Home Conditions. The breaking up of a home usually follows a long period of parent-parent bickering. These disagreements at first may take place only between the parents, but later they usually occur in the presence of and include the children. Consequently, feelings of insecurity in the affection of either or both parents are experienced by the child. If he attaches himself more strongly to one parent than to the other, he may experience criticism and severe attack from the other.

The neighborhood of the home may present numerous social stimuli that affect the child adversely. Discussions of financial difficulties between father and mother in the presence of the child may result in the latter's worrying about the great expense he is to them. The parents may expect the child to perform beyond his mental limits and thus cause him mental and emotional disturbance.

Undue Emotional Stimulation. Many emotional disturbances during childhood result from the fact that the emotional and social life of adults is far removed from that of the child. The adult may be sensitive to definite social stimuli, but he does not always recognize the fact that there are differences between the way he reacts and the way a child reacts to an apparently identical situation. The child is awed by things that are new to him but that for many years have been common experiences to the adult. For example, a child's display of emotional interest when he first recognized a banana tree as such was greeted with the response, "I thought that everyone knew a banana tree."

Nervous or high-strung parents or relatives affect the emotional behavior of a child adversely. Daily attendance at motion pictures of the "blood and thunder" type stimulates more excitement than the child may be able to endure. Likewise, the radio or the television program may arouse emotional excitement that interferes with the child's sleep, with the result that he may be irritable the next day. Overstimulation of a child's emotions usually leads to the development of unstable behavior patterns.

Thwarting of Impulses and Desires. When the circumstances are such that an individual's accustomed habit patterns are unable to satisfy an aroused motive or desire, the result is one of thwarting. If a child can use established behavior patterns successfully in responding to emotion-arousing stimuli, no thwarting exists. When impulses or desires arise in a situation for which he has no accustomed solution, the conditions are right for conflict to arise.

Significant factors that thwart human urges or motives are classified generally as (1) environmental situation (a mechanical toy fails to operate), (2) personal defect (a broken arm prevents the playing of ball), or (3) conflict with another motive (desired candy is refused by the mother). In situations such as these the child must make an adjustment to their thwarting aspects. If a feeling of conflict arises, however, the emotional element is so strong that the child seems unable to select from among his habitual responses the one that will bring about adjustment. Thwarting of impulses and desires is likely to lead to a feeling of inferiority.

MECHANISMS OF ADJUSTMENT

At first, an individual is interested primarily in self-preservation. As was stated earlier, a child's drives and urges impel him to engage in one or another form of activity. The forces of co-operation or opposition to which he is exposed, his degree of intelligence, and his varying interests contribute to the form and direction of his activities.

The mechanisms of adjustment are the habit patterns established by the child in his day-by-day living. He usually is able to satisfy his wants and urges through socially acceptable behavior. If limitations are placed upon the satisfaction of his behavior drives, however, he may attempt to vary his behavior so as to achieve desired goals. To do this he may have to develop socially less desirable attitudes and activities. The patterns thus developed represent his mechanisms of adjustment.

Newly established patterns usually reflect more or less socially desirable modes of behavior. If the individual has developed warped ideas concerning the nature of the goal to be achieved, or if he lacks ability to achieve it, he may attempt to utilize the kind of mechanism that seems to satisfy his impulse at the moment. The resulting behavior may prove to be either wholesome adjustment or maladjustment. Some of the mechanisms used by children and older persons as they achieve maturity or resolve conflicts will be discussed briefly.

Compensation. Compensatory behavior is engaged in by a child when he utilizes extra energy to develop a trait or traits for the purpose of alleviating tension caused by a real or imagined defect. Excessive activity in those functions in which the child believes he has an observable defect represents the most common and the simplest form of compensating behavior. The operation of this mechanism is exhibited in the behavior of a crippled child who becomes assertive or aggressive, of a short girl who tries to accentuate her height, or of a slow child who boasts of the superior ability of his relatives.

Introjection. The ideals, emotionalized attitudes, and opinions that a child absorbs as he lives with his parents and others come to him by way of a process called *introjection*. Social, moral, and ethical values automatically become those of the growing child as he struggles for survival in his environment. A child gets most of his ideas from others. As his experiences and educational opportunities expand, he develops values of his own and becomes less dependent upon the forces of his immediate environment.

Identification. If a child attempts to identify himself with or put himself into the place of any successful child or adult, he is utilizing the mechanism of identification. A boy's behavior is conditioned by that of his father to the extent that he is motivated to imiate his father's behavior.

Identification is considered to be the foundation of character formation. It has value when or if the child selects a desirable model for his imitative behavior and does not lose his own individuality in that of his hero. It can be undesirable if the child imitates the behavior of a socially undesirable individual or if he attempts to engage in activities or display attitudes in imitation of his model that are foreign to his ability or to his general attitude pattern.

Projection. Expression is given by the child to the mechanism of projection in one of two ways. He may attempt to place the blame for his failure upon the behavior or attitudes of another person, or he may call attention to the shortcomings of another in order that attention may be diverted from his own undesirable behavior.

190

It is easy for a child to make a mistake but not so easy for him to assume the blame. Hence, he is impelled to seek another person or force to credit with the cause of the mistake or failure. Thus, the child attributes his failure in school to the fact that the teacher selected the wrong questions; or he asserts that he got into trouble because of the actions of another child; or he states that he fell and hurt himself because a stone was in his path. These are examples of projective behavior. Another form of this mechanism is seen in the attitude of the child who cheats in an examination and then finds comfort in the thought that other pupils cheat more than he does. Self-deceit often results from the utilization of projection.

Rationalization. Another mechanism of self-deceit utilized by an individual to maintain self-respect is rationalization, the refusal to recognize the actual reason for his behavior or the actual bases of a situation. The child justifies or explains his actions by presenting reasons for his behavior which he knows to be different from those that actually motivated it. Rationalization is used for the purpose of "saving face."

It is not always easy for anyone to admit to himself or to others the true reason for his behavior. If a child fails in an activity he may announce that he was not interested in succeeding. This sour-grapes approach is characteristic of much of his rationalizing behavior. He utilizes it for the purpose of protecting himself from expected criticism of his actions. It is sometimes difficult, therefore, to obtain from children or young people straightforward answers concerning the reasons for their misdeeds.

Egocentrism. Egocentrism is characterized by behavior that has developed as a result of constant attention and praise. The child becomes accustomed to receiving attention upon demand. The temper tantrum is one of the most prominent forms of the display of egocentrism. Although egocentrism is a natural accompaniment of the very early stages of growth, a child should outgrow the egocentric attitude if he is to develop good relationships with members of his groups. Otherwise, he may experience serious frustration.

Daydreaming. Daydreaming is a normal function of the mind and in moderation is not harmful to the healthy child. Through daydreaming, imaginary satisfactions are achieved, especially those that cannot be attained in real experience. A child may experience self-satisfaction when he attains successfully in imagination those goals that are not immediately attainable in reality.

A flight of the imagination into the fanciful is not always serious. A child is in a constant state of awareness. He cannot hold his attention to the solution of one problem, however, without being stimulated to follow other unrelated ideas that may occur in his mental process. The danger is not in the mental wandering but in the fact that the child does not or cannot keep his focus of attention completely upon the problem at hand.

Daydreaming is the behavior of a child or other individual whose mind turns to matters of personal interest (rather than to those in which a parent, teacher, or other person may be interested) as goals to pursue in thought at the moment. Some daydreams have constructive and adjustive value. If the imagination is permitted to play with ideas that are basic to the realization of desired goals, these eventually may be realized in commendable achievement.

Constructive daydreaming often results in creative thinking along the lines of individual interests. Daydreams that have a basis in fact may serve as incentives toward self-realization and self-improvement. It is not harmful for a boy or a girl to dream about being popular if such thinking arouses in the young person the positive desire to do something constructive about the improvement of his existing popularity status. However, if the imagination is used as a means of escape from annoying situations, the child or young person may become separated from reality and experience serious maladjustment.

Withdrawal Mechamisms. The mechanisms of withdrawal include shyness, negativism, and regression. They may represent the beginnings of serious emotional maladjustments that can lead to mental illness.

Shyness. Retreating from a situation that is new or strange is characteristic of the behavior of most young children. This attitude is not a maladjustment unless it tends to persist and interferes eventually with social effectiveness. The child who has been over-protected, has experienced a lonely childhood, or has been too severely restricted in his behavior is likely to exhibit the characteristics of shyness.

The shy child causes no annoyance in the classroom and therefore is sometimes regarded as the especially good child. Unbeknown to the teacher, the quiet, shy child may be experiencing great emotional tension and feelings of frustration caused by his desire to participate in all the class actiities combined with the lack of sufficient courage to do so. This withdrawing attitude often is accompanied by daydreaming. Conflicts also may arise that cause still further withdrawal behavior. Unless a child is helped by an understanding adult to overcome his shyness, he may need, sometime in his later life, to be helped by a psychiatrist.

Negativism. Negativism is common during one stage of early childhood. It is a mechanism in which the chief refuses to accept a real situation, pleasant or unpleasant, and rebels against authority or adult suggestion. The child usually outgrows his behavior reaction, and no harm results. If, however, refusals persist and are accompanied by temper tantrums there is danger that negative attitudes may become part of the individual's general behavior pattern.

Regression. The mechanism of regression is characterized by the achievement of satisfaction through the use of behavior appropriate to an earlier period of development. The behavior of the individual is withdrawing to the extent that he retreats to an inferior type of adjustment rather than attempt to meet his present problems or difficulties. If a child of three or four years of age comes to resent the attention that his newborn sibling is receiving, he may insist upon help in his eating, dressing, and other activities, although he had previously been able to do these things for himself.

A child or older person who develops a feeling of insecurity in or fear of a relatively new situation may adopt a negative attitude toward it that interferes with any success that, otherwise, he might be able to achieve in it. When the regressive attitude affects all a person's relationships with his fellows, he is thereby displaying some of the symptoms of mental illness.

EMOTIONAL MALADJUSTMENT AND MENTAL ILLNESS

Severe emotional disorders and mental illness are far more prevalent than the average person realizes. The importance of the problem can be understood better, and improved measures can be taken for the prevention of mental illness, when more is known concerning the kinds and extent of psychoses (forms of mental illness) and their causes.

Seriousness of the Problem. As has been suggested earlier in this chapter, too many Americans are experiencing a more or less serious from of mental illness. Two out of five medical discharges during World War II were for extreme emotional maladjustment.

193

It has been predicted that, under existing world conditions, at least one out of ten Americans sooner or later will need psychiatric care and that, depending upon the availability of hospital beds, one out of twenty persons will be hospitalized.

Anyone may become a victim of mental illness. Hectic world conditions provide the proper setting for exciting causes to play upon the predispositions already established in the individual. At present, even a stable and well-balanced individual finds it difficult to maintain a healthy attitude toward himself and other people and conditions around him.

Predisposing and Exciting Factors. Everyone is likely to experience periods of depressing illness, feelings of thwarting, or behavior that is unhealthful. The first failure to make a satisfactory adjustment to an emotion-arousing situation is likely to lessen the power to adjust satisfactorily, and thus becomes the basis for continued failure.

The child of unstable parents may inherit possibilities of individual instability but, at the same time, he is the helpless victim of his parents' emotionally maladjusted attitudes and behavior. A child may inherit biological predispositions, or he may develop predispositions that are imposed upon him in his environment. No matter how powerful the stabilizing influences and forces outside the home may be, the effect upon a child of home conflict makes it difficult if not impossible for him to free himself completely from overemotionalized attitudes and behavior.

Inheritance, biological and social, is but one of many attributable causes of mental or emotional breakdown. Personal inability to adjust to others or to situations can be regarded as a predisposing factor. Situations may arise in a child's life, however, that act as exciting causes of more or less serious mental or emotional disorders. Some of these causes may result in no more than a temporary disturbance. Others may persist and lead to a disturbed conditions that cannot be remedied or alleviated except by way of psychiatric treatment.

Some of the more common predisposing and exciting factors that cause mental and emotional disorders are:

1. Fixed parental prejudices, denials, or shocks experienced during childhood.
2. Inability to satisfy a fundamental urge, as the sex urge, in terms of socially accepted behavior.

194

3. Abnormal anxiety, worry, boredom, or fatigue.
4. The onslaught of physiological epochs, such as puberty or the menopause.
5. Pressures associated with disturbed social, political, or economic conditions.
6. Exhaustion and toxemia indirectly produced by climatic conditions.
7. Diseases, such as syphilis.
8. Trauma or injuries, especially of the head or spine.
9. Toxic infections caused by alcohol or narcotics or by poison originating in the body, especially in the gastrointestinal tract.
10. Severe emotional shock, such as sudden fright, the death of a beloved, or the sight of the wounded or dying (as on a field of battle or in a severe accident).

Symptoms of Serious Emotional Disorders and Mental Illness. At one time or another, abnormal behavior is common to normal individuals. The symptoms of emotional disorders and of mental illness differ from this deviation of behavior in degree rather than in kind. These experiences become dangerous when they persist long enough to become fixed in the behavior pattern to such an extent that the victim of the disorder is unable to engage regularly in what may be termed normal activity.

Persisting or fixed symptoms of mental and emotional disorders can be summarized under the following general classification.

Physical Symptoms:
1. Changes in temperature, respiration, and pulse rate.
2. Dizziness, headaches, nausea, or vomiting.
3. Abnormal appetite or loss of appetite.
4. Extreme changes in weight.
5. Excessive fatigue, coughing, pupillary activity, or pain (actual or imagined).
6. Speech disturbances, writing peculiarities, or general motor incoordination.

Behavior Symptoms:
1. Decreased psychomotor activity resulting in the slowdown of motion, hesitation or indecision (abulia), rigidity, halting speech, or refusal to speak.
2. Increased psychomotor activity, impelling the individual toward constant motion, laughing, crying, shouting, or whispering.
3. Behavior that is impulsive or unduly responsive to external suggestion as shown by the persistent repetition of another's movements or words, or

by an attitude of doing the reverse of what might be expected, or by refusal to respond.

4. Constant repetition of the same act (stereotypy).

5. Unaccustomed vulgarity or profanity and peculiar mannerisms such as facial grimaces, queer movements of the hands or shoulders, and shuffling walk.

Mental Symptoms:

1. Loss of understanding or of producing language (aphasia).

2. Complete loss of memory (amnesia).

3. Loss of the power to perceive existing relationships in the environment (agnosia).

4. Distractibility, flight of ideas, delay or retardation of mental associations, and blocking of the thought processes.

5. Disturbances of perceptions such as illusions and hallucinations. An illusion is a faulty perception of an object. A hallucination is an imaginary perception that has no basis in immediate and actual sensory stimulation.

6. Phobias or strong and irrational fears that are attached to generally harmless situations.

7. Compulsions to engage in certain forms of behavior, some of which may have serious consequences. Kleptomania is the urge to take property belonging to another regardless of its value. Pyromania is the compelling desire to start fires.

8. Obsessions or fixed ideas concerning the attitudes of other people toward the patient or his own attitude toward himself or others.

9. Delusions or false beliefs that have no basis in fact, are not justified by the individual's experience, and cannot be corrected by an appeal to reason. Delusions of grandeur represent the attitude of being a person of great influence or power. Delusions of persecution represent an attitude of believing that one is the object of jealousy, hatred, and malicious influence. In melancholia the patient imagines that he is suffering from an incurable disease or has committed an unforgiveable crime.

Emotional Symptoms:

1. Exhibition of an unnatural state of elation or happiness that shows itself in dancing, singing, much laughter, and excited talking.

2. Display of a state of apathy or emotional indifference accompanied by crying, sighs, expressions of worry, and refusal to speak or to eat.

Treatment. Adults should become sufficiently acquainted with the first appearance of any of these symptoms so that they can recognize the occurrence of one or more in a child. A serious mental or emotional state of disorder could be avoided if early symptoms were recognized. Any deviation in a child's behavior that represents more than to-be-expected variation should be called to the attention of a trained psychologist or psychiatrist. It should be left to him to decide whether or not the displayed abnormal behavior is significant as a symptom of serious emotional disturbance. A layman should not attempt to administer to the patently mentally ill person therapies such as psychosomatic medicine, hydrotherapy, shock therapy, or occupational or recreational therapy.

The degree of successful rehabilitation that can be expected from the utilization of therapeutic techniques depends in large measure upon significant personal factors. Progress toward recovery is possible for the individual when his difficulty is recognized early and appropriate treatment administered. The adoption of the mental hygiene point of view and growth in scientific understanding of mental illness should be reflected in improved methods of treatment. Parents should be helped by therapists to accept the reality of the situation, so as to help the child resolve his conflicts and develop constructive attitudes toward himself in his relations with others.

SELF-TEST

True-False: Place a plus sign (+) before each statement that is true or essentially true; place a zero (0) before each statement that is false.

Multiple-Choice: Place the letter that represents the *best* answer before the number of each question.

True-False Questions

1. There is a high correlation between lack of affection given the individual in his early years and mental disorders.
2. A basic rule for maintaining good classroom discipline is good teaching.
3. Intellectual understanding creates emotional acceptance.
4. Daydreaming is psychopathic.
5. Informal classroom observation by the teacher has little diagnostic value.
6. Play therapy can be used to advantage for all children.
7. The affective side of an individual's nature results almost completely from his inner urges and desires.
8. Many emotional disturbances during childhood are caused by the fact that the adult's emotional and social behavior is far removed from that of the child.

9. It is normal and desirable for a handicapped child to receive special consideration at the expense of other children in the family.
10. Emotional stress in children almost always causes disciplinary problems.
11. In general, the longer the home is the dominant influence in a child's life, the better it is for his social development.
12. Competition with one's own record is less likely to cause emotional problems than competition with other learners.
13. A teacher's attitudes sometimes prevent him from understanding his pupils.
14. In order to retain its influence, the home should employ rigid discipline when the child enters the adolescent years.
15. The mental-hygiene-minded teacher submits himself to periodic self-evaluation, but does not necessarily undertake an evaluation of his pupils.
16. If a class is orderly, it can be assumed that its members have developed a high degree of self-discipline.
17. The child's fear of animals is almost wholly instinctive.
18. The genetic approach to child study is characterized by controlled observation over a considerable period of time.
19. The relative plasticity of the neonate presents the possibility of widely diversified responses.
20. The tempo of growth is fairly even among traits.
21. Competent observers can identify such infant emotions as love, fear, and rage.
22. If a normal and a defective gene are paired there is a tendency for the trait to be defective.
23. Tension over sex on the part of parents is a factor of minor importance in the personality adjustments of the child.
24. Ossification of the bones is a valuable index of maturation.
25. Similarities in emotional patterns among children and their parents are best explained on the basis of common genes.
26. Overprotection is certain to meet the child's need for security.
27. From the point of view of mental hygiene, the repression of emotions is more desirable than emotional outbursts.
28. The development of manipulative skills depends solely upon the number of practice periods.
29. One of the major signs of integrated personality is seen in the individual's co-ordinating his doing with his feeling.
30. Desire for prestige has little effect in motivating learning.
31. Relatively few of his basic behavior patterns are learned by an adult during his childhood.
32. The interests, wants, and attitudes of a child seldom fluctuate as he interacts with his environment.

33. Most individuals develop mentally to the extent of their capacities and aptitudes.
34. Values that relate to self arouse attitudes that are quite objective.
35. Attitudes are individual and, hence, are rarely affected by the behavior and opinion of other persons.
36. Emotional attitudes, ideals, and feelings are introjected as an individual lives with his parents and others in a society during his growing years.
37. An angry child is essentially a child struggling with a problem.
38. It is wise to meet the unhappy, defiant child with set rules of behavior.
39. A good teacher will see to it that pupils are never confronted with a problem that is not readily and successfully solved.
40. The average school child enjoys activity for which he is fitted and in which he can attain some degree of success.
41. The center of the school's mental hygiene program should be the individual classroom and not the clinic.
42. Sociodrama involves audience participation and interest in the problem.
43. Children, who at the age of seven are mentally retarded by two years, become more retarded as they grow older.
44. Differences among children in rate of social and personality growth are less than differences in physical and mental growth.
45. Children of three talk more about themselves when they are in the presence of adults than when they are with other children.
46. A child of six or seven years of age should be shifted from group to group until he finds one that he accepts and that accepts him as he is.
47. Experiments in voice training have shown that preschool training is relatively ineffective.
48. Most children cannot profit from lessons in instrumental music before the age of ten or eleven years.
49. When a child can say "one-two-three-four-five" he has learned the first meaning of numbers.
50. The autistic thinker substitutes imaginary achievement for real achievement.
51. When a two-year-old child is playing alone, better results are achieved if an adult shares in his play experiences.
52. The fetal period is the organ-forming period during prenatal development.
53. There are noticeable variations in the pitch and intensity of crying during the first two weeks of life.
54. When a child is learning to walk he should frequently be held up under the arms to lessen his fatigue.
55. A child's behavior may seem to exhibit contradictory responses.

56. Conditioned responses are stable and permanent.
57. It is now possible to establish specific physical causation in many types of mental illness.
58. Intelligence is a trait best considered apart from personality.
59. Punishment as retribution is justifiable.
60. Punishment for an offense should be discarded when a child tells the truth.
61. Most children choose their patterns of behavior deliberately.
62. In a statistical sense, negativism is normal in young children.
63. A parent should deliberately appeal to a child's affection as a motive for obedience.
64. The power to inhibit overt response is characteristic of advancing maturity.
65. In the interview, it is best to ask direct questions first, and let the interviewee tell his own story afterwards.
66. The longitudinal approach in the study of problems in child psychology is genetic in conception.
67. Paper-and-pencil tests are generally considered to be more objective than interview and observation methods.
68. The patient's conscious recollection is discarded by the psychoanalyst as a useful source of data.
69. According to the psychoanalytic theory, the individual is clearly aware of his desires and frustrations.
70. Introsepction plays a relatively small part in the psychology of early childhood.
71. Retrogression is rarely shown before the age of adolescence.
72. In aiding a maladjusted child, it is inadvisable for a teacher to make use of dream interpretation.
73. The fantasy satisfactions of children are more indirect and symbolic than those of adults.
74. As the individual matures, fear responses become, normally, more subtle.
75. Reactions to frustration involve principally the "rage" type of behavior.
76. Sex should be introduced as one of the normal aspects of life.
77. Insight arises in the solving of problems.
78. Without control of anticipatory adjustments, learning itself cannot be controlled.
79. The child needs religious experiences that accompany religious training.
80. Chinese-speaking parents transmit to their offspring an innate capacity for learning the Chinese language.
81. Learning normally increases the time taken to examine the stimulus.
82. As twins grow older they seem to grow more alike in intelligence.

83. Opposing emotional reactions take place simultaneously under strong pressure.
84. Attitudes are changed but little as a result of education.
85. Emotions involve the visceral and glandular systems of the body to a greater extent than do instincts or reflexes.
86. Some sense organs have no connections with nerves.
87. Sensations are irreducible conscious elements.
88. Pupils should be encouraged to make rapid movement when learning to write.
89. Improvements in memory means an improvement in a native capacity to retain.
90. Child-guidance clincics show that rather complete knowledge in sex education prevents undesirable behavior.
91. At first, infant sexuality is diffuse and localized in erogenous zones.
92. Sex education is largely a matter of telling the child the facts about reproduction.
93. An individual's personality patterns are relatively static.
94. Most child-guidance clinics are really parent-guidance clinics.
95. Parents, by playing one child against the other, awaken the pride of both children and spur them on to greater activity.
96. Teachers tend to overemphasize the significance of timid and asocial behavior.
97. School activity should be reduced to the play level.
98. Girls tend to be more possessive of their friends than are boys.
99. The aggressive child need not be trained to defer to the wishes and rights of others.
100. Even from a very early age, it is wise to let a child have a short vacation from his parents.

Multiple-Choice Questions

1. A well-adjusted child (a) has every wish satisfied, (b) has withstood a great deal of frustration, (c) adjusts symbolically, (d) demonstrates integrated behavior.
2. An illogical, persistent desire to perform unnecessary acts is called (a) a compulsion, (b) an illusion, (c) an obsession, (d) a phobia.
3. A socially acceptable form of defending one's ego or superego is (a) projection, (b) rationalization, (c) self-punishment, (d) arrogance.
4. The shy child can be helped to establish rapport with the group by (a) setting up special activities for him which will interest others in him and his accomplishments, (b) exposing him to a variety of activities, (c) getting him into a game of baseball, (d) all of the foregoing.

5. Of the following, which is not a characteristic of a person suffering from an anxiety neurosis? (a) morbid dread of the future, (b) self-complacency, (c) resentment, (d) indecision.

6. Thwarted egocentrism produces behavior that is most likely to develop mechanisms of (a) introjection, (b) sublimation, (c) represion, (d) attention-getting.

7. The school curriculum should place major emphasis upon (a) the present interests of the learner, (b) the acquisition of practical knowledge, (c) the meeting of present and future needs of individual learners, (d) preparation for the to-be-expected interests of the learner.

8. An adjustment program for a handicapped child should stress least (a) his likeness to normal children, (b) his special needs, (c) his dependence upon others, (d) his vocational opportunities.

9. A symptom of mental illness that is characterized by hesitation and indecision is termed (a) aphasia, (b) abulia, (c) agnosia, (d) stereotypy.

10. Significant disorders of judgment are known as (a) illusions, (b) compulsions, (c) obsessions, (d) delusions.

11. In our complex society, conflicts (a) are unimportant, (b) tend to cause failure, (c) are essential to the fullest growth and development of the individual, (d) should be encouraged.

12. Anecdotal reports are best made by (a) teachers, (b) children, (c) the principal of the school, (d) supervisors.

13. The neonate is sensitive to (a) smell, (b) pain, (c) touch, (d) sound.

14. In a child of four, which of the following is most likely to give evidence of the beginnings of fatigue? (a) cessation of play, (b) lethargy, (c) restlessness, (d) verbal expression of fatigue.

15. A preschool child talks to an inanimate object because he (a) wants to express some ideas, (b) is lonesome, (c) hopes someone will hear him, (d) likes to pretend the object is animate.

16. The most serious behavior in children of eight years or older is (a) fighting, (b) boasting, (c) blaming others, (d) disobedience.

17. Growth studies of children indicate that each child's development should be interpreted in terms of (a) his family background, (b) average growth curves for his age group, (c) his own tempo of growth, (d) a universal growth curve for his racial group.

18. A commonly used index of anatomical age is (a) ossification status, (b) height-weight ratio, (c) basal metabolism, (d) dentition status.

19. Various mental abilities (a) all continue to grow until middle age, (b) all grow at about the same rate, (c) all cease growing around 16 years of age, (d) have different rates of growth.

20. In overcoming children's fears the best procedure is to try to (a) talk them out of it, (b) ignore the fears, (c) discover the underlying causes, (d) set an example of fearlessness.

21. Emotional reactions occur only in the presence of (a) other people,

(b) strange situations, (c) perceived stimuli, (d) abnormal behavior.

22. Conflicts result from (a) satisfying inner drives, (b) thwarting inner drives, (c) following the desires of a group, (d) giving no attention to the interests of the group.

23. Social smiling usually develops (a) at birth, (b) during the first month, (c) at the end of the second month, (d) between the third and fifth months.

24. Probably the first emotional patterns to develop are (a) distress and delight, (b) fear and anger, (c) elation and satisfaction, (d) jealousy and disgust.

25. Imaginary companions are most prevalent between the years of (a) one and two, (b) two and three, (c) five and six, (d) twelve and thirteen.

26. A child who shows jealousy has usually experienced (a) early emotional conditioning, (b) frustration and interference, (c) normal emotional maturation, (d) a recognition of his role in the social group.

27. A widely used technique for measuring the effects of maturation and learning upon children's behavior is the (a) controlled experimental method, (b) intensive case study method, (c) cross-section test method, (d) age-group method.

28. Attention span refers to (a) the length of time one can attend to anything, (b) the shifting of attention from one thing to another, (c) the number of things one can attend to at a time, (d) the ability to rule out distractions.

29. With respect to the color sense, normal infants (a) respond to color at birth, (b) respond to color but not to brightness, (c) are three months old before they respond to color, (d) respond only to certain colors by the age of six months.

30. The language errors of preschool children are due mostly to (a) their inability to think, (b) insufficient help from parents (c) the poor English used by adults, (d) their immaturity.

31. Bilingualism means that (a) both parents speak one language, (b) twins speak a language different from that of their parents, (c) children confuse several languages with each other, (d) two languages are spoken in the home.

32. Evidence supports the conclusion that young children acquire most of their racial prejudices from (a) contact with adults who show prejudice, (b) contacts with adolescents who show antagonistic attitudes, (c) contact with children of other races, (d) experiences gained through the radio and television.

33. Which of the following is not a congenital factor that may produce abnormalities in the offspring?   (a) malnutrition, (b) infection, (c) endocrine imbalance, (3) chromosomal defect.

34. By the age of three months the infant is not able to (a) turn over from side to side, (b) co-ordinate the eyes to be able to see objects several

feet away, (c) hold head upright unsupported, (d) crawl across the floor.

35. Faulty food habits may be the result of (a) underweight, (b) overweight, (c) poor training, (d) heredity.

36. The primary factor in learning to walk is (a) exercise, (b) desire to walk, (c) training, (d) maturation.

37. The mental age of a child (a) is equal to the I.Q., (b) increases with age, (c) correlates perfectly with physiological age, (d) corresponds with the chronological age.

38. More maturation than learning is shown when a year-old child (a) picks up an object with pincer movement, (b) refuses to swallow food, (c) walks to the door when the bell rings, (d) says "Da-da" on sight of a man.

39. If a child of three months stiffens his back on the approach of an adult, such behavior should be considered to be evidence of (a) mass activity, (b) social development, (c) cephalocaudal development, (d) a subcortical level of response.

40. The most important conditioning factor in children's learning to accept themselves is (a) the affection of their parents, (b) popularity with their classmates, (c) their success in school achievement, (d) a permissive attitude by parents toward the child's wants.

41. The most frequent cause of disobedience among children seven to nine years old is the (a) desire to gain new experiences, (b) failure to remember past admonitions, (c) inability to understand parents' explanations, (d) wish to gain attention.

42. In the case of a shy child the rest of the children should be (a) praised for coaxing him to join them, (b) criticized if they fail to invite him to join them, (c) told to ignore him, (d) urged to invite him to join them.

43. During preschool years the play activity is characteristically (a) exploratory, (b) social, (c) competitive, (d) antisocial.

44. If a child of nine should begin to use vulgar words (a) such speech should be ignored, (b) any suitable punishment may be used, (c) the parent should repeat such expressions to shame him, (d) a substitute expression should be given.

45. When a child of five dismembers a toy engine, the behavior should be viewed as (a) wholesome curiosity, (b) ignorance of the value of property, (c) destructive tendency, (d) creativity.

46. The child's tendency to be loquacious rests primarily upon the interacting influences of maturation and (a) emotional stability, (b) social contracts, (c) auditory acruity, (d) physical development.

47. In manipulative experiences a kindergarten child of low intelligence will reveal (a) low powers of concentration, (b) more skill than a child of superior intelligence, (c) destructiveness, (d) no particular interests.

48. In the process of arriving at a concept, which of the following is the

first step? (a) abstraction, (b) differentiation, (c) generalization, (d) hypothesizing.

49. One of the most important conditions of children's security is (a) family status, (b) consistency, (c) overprotection, (d) lack of restraint.

50. The utilization of competition as a means of motivating learning activities (a) is undesirable because it tends to develop attitudes of frustration, (b) yields better results among older children if it takes the form of competition between learners, (c) should lead to friendly rivalry among children of the same relative ability to perform, (d) should be fostered by granting extrinsic awards.

SELECTED REFERENCES

Angrilli, A., and L. Helfat, *Child Psychology.* Barnes & Noble, 1981.

Ambron, S.R., *Child Development,* 2nd ed. Holt, Rinehart and Winston, 1978.

Biehler, R.F., *Child Development: An Introduction,* 2nd ed. Houghton-Mifflin Company, 1981.

Brunck, J.W., *Child and Adolescent Development.* Wiley, 1975.

Crow, L.D., *Psychology of Childhood and Adolescence.* Exposition Press, 1978.

Crow, L.D., *Personality.* Prinit Press, 1978.

Crow, L.D., *Development of Self-Discipline.* Prinit Press, 1980.

Crow, L.D. & A. Crow, *General Psychology.* Littlefield, Adams, 1972.

Crow, L.D. & A. Crow, *How To Study.* Macmillan, 1963.

Dill, J.R., *Child Psychology in Contemporary Society.* Allyn, 1978.

Elkin, F., and G. Handel, *Child and Society.* Random House, 1978.

Fong, B. & M. Resnick, *Child: Development through Adolescence.* A-W, 1980

Harvey, G., *Child Psychology.* Wiley, 1975.

Homans, P., *Childhood and Selfhood.* Bucknell University Press, 1978.

Hurlock, E.B., *Child Growth & Development,* 5th ed. McGraw-Hill, 1977.

Hymovich, D.P. & R. Chamberlin, *Child and Family Development.* McGraw-Hill, 1980.

Jimenez, S.L., *Child Bearing: A Guide for Pregnant Parents.* Prentice-Hall, 1980.

Lipsitt, L.P., *Child Development.* Scott Foreman, 1979.

Manning, S.A., *Child and Adolescent Development.* McGraw-Hill, 1977.

Medinnus, G.R., & R.C. Johnson, *Child and Adolescent Psychology,* 2nd ed. Wiley, 1976.

Meyer, W.J., & J.B. Dusek, *Child Psychology: A Developmental Perspective.* Heath, 1979.

Mussen, P.H. et al, *Child Development and Personality,* 5th Ed. Harper & Row, 1979.

Pinkerton, P., *Childhood Disorders: A Psychomatic Approach.* Columbia University Press, 1975.

Rogers, D., *Child Psychology,* 2nd ed. Brooks-Cole, 1977.

Sarafine, E.P., & J.W. Armstrong., *Child and Adolescent Development.* Scott Foresman, 1980.

Saul, L.J., *Childhood Emotional Patterns & Maturity.* Van Nostrand Reinhold, 1980.

Sheppard, S.R., & R.H. Willoughby, *Child Behavior: Learning and Development.* Random House, 1975.

Shipman, M., *Childhood: A Sociological Perspective.* Humanities, 1972.

Spencer, T.D., and N. Kass, *Perspective in Child Psychology.* McGraw-Hill, 1970.

Stone, J.L., & J. Church, *Childhood and Adolescence: A Psychology of the Growing Person.* Random House, 1979.

ANSWERS TO SELF-TEST QUESTIONS

True-False				Multiple-Choice	
1. +	26. 0	51. 0	76. +	1. d	26. b
2. +	27. 0	52. +	77. +	2. a	27. c
3. 0	28. 0	53. +	78. +	3. b.	28. a
4. 0	29. +	54. 0	79. +	4. d	29. c
5. 0	30. 0	55. +	80. 0	5. b	30. d
6. +	31. 0	56. 0	81.0	6. d	31. d
7. 0	32. 0	57. 0	82.0	7. c	32. a
8. +	33. 0	58. 0	83. 0	8. c	33. d
9. 0	34. 0	59. 0	84. 0	9. b	34. d
10. 0	35. 0	60. 0	85. +	10. d	35. c
11. 0	36. +	61. 0	86. 0	11. c	36. d
12. +	37. +	62. +	87. +	12. a	37. b
13. +	38. 0	63. 0	88. 0	13. d	38. a
14. 0	39. 0	64. +	89. 0	14. c	39. b
15. 0	40. +	65. 0	90. 0	15. a	40. a
16. 0	41. +	66. +	91. +	16. c	41. a
17. o	42. +	67. +	92. 0	17. c	42. d
18. +	43. 0	68. 0	93. 0	18. d	43. a
19. +	44. 0	69. 0	94. +	19. d	44. d
20. 0	45. 0	70. +	95. 0	20. c	45. a
21. 0	46. +	71. 0	96. 0	21. c	46. b
22. 0	47. +	72. +	97. 0	22. b	47. a
23. 0	48. 0	73. +	98. +	23. d	48. d
24. +	49. 0	74. +	99. 0	24. a	49. b
25. +	50. +	75. +	100. +	25. b	50. c

INDEX